DIRECTORS' DUTIES AND RESPONSIBILITIES IN THE EUROPEAN COMMUNITY

DIRECTORS' DUTIES *and* RESPONSIBILITIES *in the* EUROPEAN COMMUNITY

A Country by Country Guide

Compiled by
JANE WHITTAKER

Edited by
ALEX RONEY

MACFARLANES

LONDON *of* CHAMBER
COMMERCE AND INDUSTRY

KOGAN PAGE

First published in 1992

Kogan Page Limited
120 Pentonville Road
London N1 9JN

British Library Cataloguing in Publication Data

A CIP record for this book is available from the
British Library.

ISBN 0 7494 0307 1

CONTENTS

FOREWORD

This authoritative book of reference, detailing the liabilities and duties of company directors, fills a gap which has certainly been sensed by many companies trading in the European Community and, more especially, investing within the Community. Whatever is said or proposed about a European company law, national company law is likely to remain the standard structure of company law in the member countries of the Community well into the future. By no means everything is governed by EC directives, or is likely to be. Important differences will remain, just as they do as between the 50 states of the USA. National company law will, of course, incorporate the various relevant EC directives, but national law will remain the basis.

Most businesspeople will be unfamiliar with company law in other EC countries. There may be a tendency to assume that the duties and liabilities of directors will be like those of one's own country. Here is the opportunity to make a rapid check whether that is true and if, as will often be the case, it is not, to obtain easy access to the correct information.

A manual of this nature requires in its preparation a high degree of detailed information and expertise. The authors of this valuable compendium are, therefore, to be congratulated on producing a book which answers so many questions central to investment and trading decisions. For example, how are companies structured in the 12 member countries, how much is law, how much is left to be determined by the articles of association, and how much is convention? Who can and cannot be a director? What duties are placed on directors and to what liabilities are they subject, for example in the event of a breach of the law by their subordinates? Can companies or only individuals commit crimes? What, if any, are the limits of personal liability? What does the law require in respect of employee representation?

These are only examples of the information that can be derived from this book. Company directors will find an increasing need to become familiar with the law and practices of our partner countries. Here, conveniently, is what they will want to know.

Edmund Dell, 1992

INTRODUCTION

THE SCOPE OF THIS BOOK

There is no doubt that the creation of a single market in the 12 countries of the EC is creating more and greater opportunities for cross-border business arrangements. This means that it is vital that businesspeople, whatever they do, have a basic understanding of the operation of companies in various member states, and the duties and responsibilities they would incur as directors under the different regimes.

The purpose, therefore, of this book is to provide that basic understanding by way of a guide to the general provisions in each member state.

To do this in as clear a way as possible, we have set the information out in a question-and-answer format. To make appropriate comparisons between the different systems possible, we have formulated a set of standard questions. However, wherever necessary, to make the text easy to understand, extra questions and answers have been put in.

The questions cover the structure of companies in the EC, and the role of directors. It is hoped that the book will be used as an introduction to understand the basic national frameworks in operation, and will serve as a useful checklist of the main issues that arise.

It is emphasised that should an individual, a company or its directors intend to set up in another member state, then it will be necessary to obtain advice from a firm specialising in that area for a more comprehensive analysis and for detailed legal and taxation advice.

It is also important to remember and take account of the fact that there is, and will continue to be fast-moving developments in company and related legal provisions throughout the Community. This book represents the state of the law applicable in December 1991.

It only remains to say that the book has been created to meet a perceived need, at the initiative of the London Chamber of Commerce and Industry, and of Macfarlanes, a firm of London solicitors, who themselves contributed the chapter on English companies. Macfarlanes, largely through the efforts of Jane Whittaker, have co-ordinated the responses from well-known law firms in each of the member states, and we are most grateful to the partners and lawyers within these firms who have made such valuable contributions. That was the hardest task. I merely had the pleasure of editing the contributions. We are sure you will find it useful.

Alex Roney, March 1992

BELGIUM

Jacques Derenne

What are the main types of company which exist in Belgium?
There are two main forms of company in Belgium which are under an obligation to appoint directors*:

- the 'Société Anonyme' (SA) or 'Naamloze Vennootschap' (NV);
- the 'Société Privée à Responsabilité Limitée; (SPRL) or 'Besloten Vennootschaap met Beperkte Aansprakelijkheid' (BVBA) private limited company.

Is the Société Anonyme/Naamloze Vennootschap a public company?
The SA/NV is a public company and as such is a legal entity. It may be compared with the English plc. Its shares may be quoted on the Stock Exchange. This form of company is mostly chosen by larger businesses and is often suitable for Belgian subsidiaries of foreign companies.

What about the private limited liability company structure?
The SPRL/BVBA is a private company and as such is a legal entity. This form of company is mostly used by smaller businesses and family-owned enterprises. SPRL/BVBA may be incorporated by one or more individuals. Its shares may not be quoted on the Stock Exchange as the SPRL/BVBA may not offer its shares to the general public.

What about the legal framework for both types of company?
The legal framework for Belgian companies, originally contained in the Belgian Code de Commerce, was modified in 1935 by a Royal Decree, the

---

*For the purpose of this text, 'directors' must be understood under Belgian law as 'administrateurs', ie members of the board of directors ('Conseil d'administration'). 'Administrateurs' must be contrasted with 'directeurs' (managers) who are members of the Management Committee ('Comité de direction'). 'Directeurs' (managers) are employed persons which presupposes a relationship of subordination. 'Administrateurs' (directors), on the other hand, are not employed by the company and their liability is less limited than that of managers. Indeed, Article 18 of the law on the employment contract (law dated 3 July 1978) provides that employees are only responsible for their gross misconduct. This text only concerns directors ('administrateurs'), although certain directors may of course be appointed both as managers ('directeurs') and directors. In such a case, they are managing directors ('administrateurs – directeurs').

'Loi commerciale sur les sociétés' (LCS). This modified several laws now usually referred to as the 'Co-ordinated company laws' (Gecoordoneerde wetten op de Handels-Vennootschappen/Lois Coordonnéés sur les Sociétés Commerciales). Since then, the law has been subject to amendment, especially to introduce EC law into Belgian national law. The provisions for the SA/NV are contained in section IV of Title IX of Book I (Articles 26 to 104bis) and those for SPRL/BVBA in Section VI of Title IV of Book I (Articles 116 to 140 quater).

The LCS was recently amended by a law of 18 July 1991 (*Belgian Official Gazette* of 26 July, 1991) as far as takeover bids are concerned. Some amendments concern the liability of directors.

MANAGEMENT OF A SA/NV

What are the requirements for the management structure of a SA/NV?
A SA/NV is managed by a board of directors ('conseil d'administration' or 'raad van bestuur'). This board undertakes all transactions which are necessary to carry out the company's objectives. The board represents the company. The day-to-day business of the company is usually carried on by one or more managing directors ('administrateur délégué' or 'afgevaardigde-bestuurder') who may be members of the board.

Although the company does not have a supervisory board (as is the case for instance in a German AG), one or more supervisors (commissaires/commissarissen) must be elected by the general meeting. If the company is a company undertaking a public offering of shares, one supervisor must be a member of the Institut des Réviseurs d'Entreprise/Instituut der Bedrijfsrevisoren.

The supervisors must inspect and audit certain major transactions of the corporation, for example increasing the capital of the company.

How many directors must a SA/NV have?
A SA/NV must have at least three directors ('administrateurs'/'bestuurders'). The number of the other members of the management of a company is not specified by law, but the law states that the day-to-day business of a SA/NV may be run by one or several persons.

Who can be a director in a SA/NV?
No special qualifications are required for directors of public companies. Thus, anybody with full legal capacity may be a director. However, certain professions are disqualified under the law, such as notaries, judges and civil

servants. A legal entity, ie another company, may be a director. When another company is a director, it must be represented either by its board of directors or by one or more directors vested with the power of general representation (in accordance with Article 54, indent 5, LCS). Alternatively, as far as the function of the director company may be part of its day-to-day management, it may be represented by a delegate from among those responsible for the day-to-day management of the company.

Must members of the board be shareholders of the company?
No, members of the board of directors need not be shareholders of the company.

Non-Belgians may be directors of a Belgian company, but they need a special 'professional card' (carte professionnelle/beroepskaart), unless they are a Dutch or Luxembourg national. These cards are obtained from the Minister of the 'Classes Moyennes'. An exemption is granted to nationals of other EC member states. Directors who are resident abroad must elect domicile at the registered office of the company in respect of all relations with the company.

The registered office of the company must be in Belgium.

Who is excluded from being a director?
The following persons are excluded from being a director:

- undischarged bankrupts and persons who have been imprisoned for a serious crime (Royal Decree No 22 of 24 October 1934, as amended by the Act of 4 August 1978);
- judges;
- civil servants;
- notaries;
- auditors of the company.

Who appoints a director?
The directors of a SA/NV are appointed in two different ways which depend on the time of appointment:

- on establishment of the company the directors are appointed by the initial shareholders (founders) in the articles of association;
- at any other stage, the directors are appointed by shareholders' resolution in general meeting.

The directors appointed must accept their functions, and their election must be published in the *Belgian Official Gazette (Moniteur Belge)*.

For how long can a director be appointed?
The directors may not be appointed for a period exceeding six years.

What is the relationship between the company and the director?
The director/company relationship is regarded by law as a 'mandate'. This means that the director has to respect the extent of the power granted to him or her and he or she must act on behalf of the company. However, this rule is only applicable to the relationship between the company and the director.

What is the relationship vis-à-vis third persons?
As creditors and other third parties need protection from restrictions of the director's power, the director acts as an organ of the company and, with effect to third persons, represents the company without regard to any internal restrictions of his or her powers. (Act of 6 March 1973 and Council Directive EEC/68/151 of 9 March 1968).

What about service contracts?
It is debatable as to whether or not the director/business manager may have a service contract with the company. This question is not resolved by the relevant legislation, but jurisprudence suggests that a service contract requires the relationship of employer and employee which does not arise in the case of a director.

How is the director rewarded?
There are no special rules concerning the rewards of directors under Belgian law. The law only states that the directors may execute their office with or without a remuneration. The articles of association decide whether or not the director shall receive a remuneration. They also fix the amount and form of the director's rewards. As there is no legal framework regarding the remuneration of directors, the 'Commission bancaire et financière' (the financial and banking commission) made a statement regarding the abuse by companies in relation to directors' remuneration. Usually, the following forms of remuneration are agreed:

- a profit share;
- 'jetons de présence' as rewards for attendance at meetings;
- a participation in the turnover;
- a fixed salary;
- directors may also receive rewards in kind.

Are there any restrictions on benefits which the director can receive from the company?
The director can receive loans and guarantees from the company following board approval.

What are the tax and social security contributions to be paid by a director?
Tax
The tax treatment of directors' fees and salaries depends on whether or not the director is resident as opposed to domiciled in Belgium.

Individuals are deemed to be resident in Belgium when they are registered with the Civil Register, unless the contrary has been proved. However, for tax purposes, the tax administration will consider any factual elements proving the reality of the residence.

Companies which do not have their registered office, main establishment or place of management in Belgium are considered as non-resident companies in Belgium.

Resident directors
Directors are taxed in Belgium in one of the income tax categories depending on the kind of remuneration granted to them.

A 5 per cent lump sum deduction may replace all deductible expenses and charges, with the exception of social security contributions. Foreign income taxes are considered to be expenses and are deductible from gross income before applying the lump sum deduction of 5 per cent.

Non-resident directors
A special tax status as provided for in the Tax Circular of 8 August 1983 may be granted upon request to non-resident directors who are temporarily assigned by a foreign company in Belgium. This status consists principally of the exemption from personal income tax of a variety of expatriate allowances, representing the special costs of working and living temporarily in Belgium. Such non-taxable items include cost of living allowances, housing allowances, tuition and home leave grants, as well as tax equalisation payments. (However, the tax exemption may not exceed 450,000BFr. for executives working for productive enterprises, and 1,200,000 BFr. for executives working for control or co-ordination offices, or scientific research centres or laboratories qualified as so-called 'co-ordination centres').

Thereafter tax is payable at the current rate for non-residents.

Social security contributions
Both resident and non-resident directors are subject to social security regulations for self-employed persons and must pay contributions under this scheme. Such contributions must even be paid by directors who do not receive fees or any other remuneration.

Exceptions
No such contributions need to be paid when the director does not receive any remuneration as a director from the Belgian company and

- the articles of the company stipulate especially that directors' services will not be remunerated; or
- the general meeting decides that directors' services shall not be remunerated.

If the directors are employees of the company, they may be subject to the social security scheme for employees.

What is the basis of a director's authority?
The powers of a director are mainly derived from two sources:

- the law specifies the powers of directors in s54 of the LCS
- the articles of association may also control the scope of the directors' powers. However, restrictions are only enforceable as between the company and the director – third parties are not subject to such restrictions.

What are the powers of a director?
The board of directors of a Belgian company has three main powers:

- the board is entitled to run the business of the company and to undertake all acts necessary to ensure that the company's objectives are achieved;
- the board may represent the company in all matters, including litigation;
- the board of directors must procure the preparation of annual accounts for submission to the general meeting.

May the powers of the board be delegated?
Yes. The board of directors may delegate the power to run the day-to-day business affairs of the company to another person. If this person is a member of the board, that person will be called 'administrateur délégué' or 'administrateur directeur'. If the power is granted to a third person, then that person is known as a 'directeur général'.

The delegation may only be made for the running of day-to-day business affairs and this includes all acts which are necessary to maintain the company's business.

Like the members of the board, the person to whom the power is delegated is an 'organ' of the company.

May the powers of the board be delegated to several persons?

Yes. The delegation may be to one or more persons under Article 54, indent 4 of the LCS.

How are the powers of a director restricted?

The powers of a director can be restricted in several ways.

- The director may not act where the competence of another organ of the company is required. Thus, he or she may not undertake the following acts reserved by law to the shareholders for decisions in general meeting:

  — appointment of the members of the board of directors and the auditors;
  — the approval of the annual accounts;
  — the decision as to the allocation of profits;
  — modification of the authorised share capital and the articles of association;
  — authorisation of the company's acts.

  The above restrictions are enforceable by third parties.

- The articles of association may provide for further restrictions which are not enforceable against third persons – for example, the distribution of powers between the administrators according to specific functions (ie finance, property, marketing etc) (Article 54, indent 3, LCS).

- As a general principle, Belgian law provides that the company is represented by all the directors collectively, but the articles of association may provide otherwise. Article 54, indent 4, LCS, provides that articles may give a general power of representation to one or more directors. This clause is, as an exception to Article 54, indent 3, LCS, enforceable against third parties, provided certain specific publicity requirements, set out in Article 10, LCS, are met. These include the filing of the instrument conferring the power of representation on a director with the Commercial Court Registry and the publication of this instrument in the Annexes of the *Belgian Official Gazette*).

- If there is a conflict of interest, a director is not allowed to act or to vote. If the director does act (for example, if he or she enters into a contract with the company in his or her personal capacity), the decision is not void but the director is liable for any damages. It should be noted that Article 60, LCS, which governs conflicts of interest, has been replaced by a new text contained in the law of 18 July 1991. The new Article 60, LCS, provides *inter alia* that if the conflict of interest only arises because the director in question is on the board of directors of more than one related company, then his or her vote will not be void. Article 60, LCS also sets out specific procedures relating to the adoption of operations or decisions where there is a conflict of interest.

The company may choose to annul such operations or decisions if they have given the director involved an advantage which is detrimental to the company. If this occurs, the director must compensate the company for the advantage received. It should be noted, however, that any such annulment is not enforceable against third persons (Article 13, law of 19 July 1991, replacing Article 60, LCS).

- Although the board of directors is not subject to control by a supervisory board, the transactions of the company are controlled by special supervisors known as commissaires/commissarissen.

What are the duties of the commissaires/commissarissen?

Their obligation is to examine the annual accounts including the balance sheet and the profit and loss accounts on the basis of a report established every six months by the members of the board of directors.

Do commissaires/commissarissen need a special qualification?

Yes. The supervisors must be members of the National Institute of Supervisors. They are appointed by the general assembly of the shareholders from the members of the National Institute of Supervisors. There must be at least one supervisor.

What are the duties of a director?

The directors must:

- carry on the business in a diligent and proper way;
- establish the annual accounts in a correct manner;
- respect the commercial companies code; and
- respect their obligations arising from the articles of association.

What is the liability system for directors?

The extent of liability differs depending on whether the director is a founder member, a subscriber or only a director. Some special liabilities exist in the case of founder members and subscribers, including liability for a share capital which is 'manifestly insufficient' where a company becomes insolvent within three years of its incorporation (Article 35 of the LCS).

As far as directors are concerned, their special and general liabilities are set out below.

What are the penalties for a breach of duty by a board director?
The law governing the liability of directors of a SA/NV is contained in Article 62 of the LCS and the Co-ordinated Company Laws. Directors may incur general liability in the following cases.

- Under Article 62 of the LCS for mismanagement of the company by the director. Each director is personally liable for any mismanagement which results in damage to the company. The civil claim may be made by the company represented by the members of the board of management or by a specially authorised person. The company, in a general meeting, must decide whether, and in what form, legal action should be taken, ie a group of shareholders acting on its own is not entitled to decide on the appropriate legal action. Third parties are only entitled to initiate proceedings against a director if the company fails to serve any proceedings against him or her.
- For breach of company law or of the articles of association by the director in the performance of his or her duties (Article 62(2) of the LCS). In this case the directors are jointly liable to the company and third parties.
- For the breach of the company law provisions relating to the increase of share capital. Any breach of these rules results in the joint and several liability of all directors.
- Directors are responsible for torts against the company and third parties (Article 1382 of the Civil Code).

A new Article 66bis was introduced into the LCS by the law of 18 July 1991. This new article provides for the following procedures against directors under Article 62, LCS:

- shareholders can now bring a so-called social action ('action sociale') against directors. The decision to bring such an action is taken by the shareholders in general meeting who may authorise one or more of their number to conduct this action; and
- under specific conditions of procedure, the same action may be lodged by minority shareholders (ie those having a minimum of 1 per cent of

the votes attached to the issued shares, or those having shares representing a minimum of 50 million Bfr).

In addition to the circumstances listed above in which a director may face general liability, a special liability may exist if a company becomes insolvent (Article 63ter of LCS) (see opposite page).

Can directors be exonerated from their general and special liability?
The articles of association cannot exonerate directors from their general and special liability. However, the shareholders in general meeting may by resolution exempt the directors from their responsibility for acts incurring general liability as provided by Article 62 of the LCS.

Is a company liable for mismanagement by its director?
Yes. The company is liable for acts of directors committed in relation to the mismanagement of the company, including torts.

Are directors jointly and severally liable?
Article 62 of the Co-ordinated Company Laws LCS provides for the liability of directors in accordance with the general law and for negligent mismanagement.

The general law provides for joint and several liability in two situations:

- negligence arising out of the joint acts of several persons;
- negligence arising out of the independent acts of several individuals which together cause the damage.

For there to be joint and several liability there must be a judgment of the court to that effect.

Negligent mismanagement resulting from infringement of the LCS or the articles of association also gives rise to joint and several liability. Directors may only escape such liability where they did not actually participate in the infringement and:

- they were not negligent in taking the course of action that they did; and
- notice of the infringement was given to the general assembly immediately following the date on which they became aware of the infringement.

What is the scope of product liability in Belgium and who is responsible for it?
Under Belgian law, there is no general statute concerning product liability. However, according to the jurisprudence, there is a general principle of

product liability contained in the Civil Code (with the result that, in general, the *owner* of the product is responsible). The EC directive of 25 July 1985 on product liability is incorporated in Belgian law by the law of 25 February, 1991, *Belgian Office Gazette* dated 22 March 1991.

What are the consequences of company insolvency for directors?

If the insolvency results in the director being charged with a criminal offence then the director will be disqualified from any sort of commercial activity whatsoever for an indefinite period.

There is also the possibility that Belgian law will impute the insolvency to a director without holding him or her criminally liable for it. If this is the case then the director may be disqualified as above, but the period of the disqualification will be limited; the minimum period is three months and the maximum ten years. The duration will be fixed by the court.

If neither of these two situations applies, there can be no disqualification of a director under Belgian law.

An exception to the general principle that directors are not liable for the debts of the company was introduced by a law in 1978 which made the directors liable for any insufficiency of assets in the case of insolvency if this insufficiency was caused by their serious default.

How does an individual cease to be a director?

The mandate of a director ceases for the following reasons:

- death – the death of a member of the board of directors must be announced and made public by the board in the annexes of the *Moniteur Belge*;
- bankruptcy of the director or where the director has been found by the court to be unable to pay his debts (ie 'cessation de payement');
- resignation or dismissal of a director – a director of a SA/NV may resign at any time provided his resignation does not constitute a fault, ie because it is 'unreasonable';
- termination of the director's office.

When can a director of a SA/NV resign or be dismissed?

The shareholders in a general meeting may dismiss a director at any stage. This even applies to directors appointed by the articles of association. The dismissal can take effect without any reasons being given. There is no right of indemnity. The dismissal or resignation is effective from the time of its announcement.

21

MANAGEMENT OF A SPRL/BVBA

What about the management structure of a SPRL/BVBA?
The SPRL/BVBA is managed by one or more managing directors ('gérants' or 'zaakvoerders'). The day-to-day business is run by either the managing directors or a chief executive.

Do commissaires/commissarissen have to be appointed?
Yes. They must be appointed in a SPRL/BVBA if the company has more than five shareholders. As in the case of a NV/SA, they are entitled to examine the transactions of the company.

How many managing directors must a SPRL/BVBA have?
Unlike in the case of a SA/NV, the SPRL/BVBA only requires one managing director. If a SPRL/BVBA has several managing directors, these act as a 'collège de gestion', a collective organ.

Who can be a managing director?
There are no special requirements as to the qualification of a managing director.

Who is excluded from being a managing director?
The same persons as in the case of a director are excluded from being a managing director, as follows:

- undischarged bankrupts and persons who have been imprisoned for a serious crime (Royal Decree No 22 of 24 October 1934, as amended by the Act of 4 August 1978);
- judges;
- civil servants;
- notaries;
- auditors of the company.

Who appoints a managing director?
There are two different ways of appointing the managing director:

- he may be appointed by the initial shareholders in the articles of association or;
- during the financial year, he may be appointed by the shareholders in a general meeting.

How long is the term of office of a managing director?

The managing director may be appointed either for a fixed term or for an uncertain period. If no time limit is set, the managing director is regarded as being appointed for the duration of the company or until retirement date.

The election of the managing director must be published in the Annex of the *Belgian State Gazette (Moniteur Belge)*.

What is the relationship between the company and the managing director?

The managing director is an 'organ' of the company. As the head of the corporation, he or she runs the business of the company. Whether or not the managing director can at the same time be an employee of the company is presently under discussion in Belgium. However, as the service agreement requires an element of subordination under the management of the company, this would seem to be unlikely.

How is the managing director rewarded?

If the managing director is to be rewarded, this will be provided for in the articles and may take the form of a fee, or sharing of profit, or any other form of remuneration as set out in the articles.

Are there any restrictions on benefits which the managing director can receive from the company?

Any restrictions on benefits the managing director may receive from the company are subject to the articles or to the decision of the general assembly.

What are the tax and social security contributions to be paid by a managing director?

The tax and social security contributions of a managing director are similar to those of a director of an SA/NV, in that the regime under which they are taxed depends on whether or not they are employees of the company.

From where does a managing director derive his authority?

- The law defines the powers of a managing director in s130, LCS
- The powers may be further determined by the articles of association and other contractual agreements.

What are the powers of a managing director?

Like the board of directors of a SA/NV, the managing director of a SPRL/BVBA has appropriate authority to run the day-to-day business and represent the company *vis-à-vis* third persons. As the office of managing director is personal, a managing director may not delegate his or her powers to a third person, although powers for special acts and tasks may be delegated to third persons by the managing director.

How are the powers of a managing director restricted?

As in the case of a SA/NV, the powers of a managing director are limited by the articles of association and should not impinge on the competence of another organ of the company. Further, where there is a conflict of interest, his or her powers may be limited – and the other managing directors or person specifically appointed may decide whether or not the managing director concerned may act.

Unlike the director of a board of directors, the managing director is not obliged to act together with another managing director if several managing directors are appointed. However, the articles of association may provide that only joint representation by the managing directors of the company is valid. If this is made public (under the same procedure as for a SA/NV under Articles 54 and 10, LCS), this restriction is enforceable against third persons (under Article 130, LCS).

What are the duties of a managing director?

Like the director of a SA/NV, the managing director is obliged to carry on the business in a diligent and proper way. He or she must also respect all the obligations imposed on him or her as a managing director by the law or by the articles of association.

What are the penalties for breach of duties by a managing director?

The liability of a managing director is almost the same as for a director of a SA/NV. The same rules as to general liability and special liability in insolvency are applicable. However, regarding the special liability in a company's insolvency, it should be noted that the corresponding provisions are only applicable to a SPRL/BVBA if they had a turnover of at least 25 million BFr and if the total of the balance sheet amounts to at least 15 million BFr during the financial year prior to the initiation of the bankruptcy proceedings.

Is a company liable for the default of its managing director?

As in the case of a director, the company is liable for the default of its managing director and this includes tortious acts.

What about product liability of managing directors?
As for a SA/NV (see page 20).

What are the consequences of company insolvency for managing directors?
As for a SA/NV (see page 21).

How does an individual cease to be a managing director?
As in the case of a director, the office of a managing director may be terminated for the following reasons:

* death;
* bankruptcy or 'cessation de payement' by the managing director ('cessation de payement' is the first stage in bankruptcy and involves proving that the individual is in debt and that the situation is deteriorating);
* resignation or dismissal of a managing director;
* termination of the managing director's office.

How may the managing director be dismissed?
Where the managing director of a SPRL/BVBA is appointed by the articles of association, such appointment is only revocable in the following cases:

* the articles of association provide for the dismissal of the managing director;
* the managing director may be dismissed by a unanimous vote of the shareholders (partners) of the SPRL/BVBA;
* the managing director may be dismissed by a qualified majority of the shareholders in general meeting (ie the majority necessary to amend the articles) in the case of dismissal for a significant reason such as gross misconduct (eg infringement of the articles, bankruptcy etc);
* by reason of his or her stated period of office coming to an end.

Where the managing director of a SPRL/BVBA is appointed by the general meeting, he or she may be dismissed at any stage without notice by a simple majority of the shareholders.

If the managing director is only appointed for a restricted period, then dismissal prior to the expiry of such a period is subject to justifiable cause.

The dismissal of a managing director must be made public in the *Official Gazette* and where appropriate this should state the reason for dismissal.

Is the managing director able to resign?
Yes.

DENMARK

Steen Lassen

What are the main types of companies in Denmark?
There are two forms of companies in Denmark.

- A public company ('aktieselskab'). Only a public company must, and indeed is authorised to, use the word 'aktieselskab' or an abbreviation thereof (A/S or AKTS), together with its name. This structure is normally used by large enterprises which require a large capital base.
- A private company ('anpartsselskab'). A private company must, and is solely authorised to, use the word 'anpartsselskab' or the abbreviation 'ApS', together with its name. This structure is usually chosen by smaller businesses.

In the following explanation, the rules will be described first for public companies and then for private companies.

What about the Danish company legislation?
Public companies

Public companies are subject to the Danish Public Companies Act ('aktieselskabsloven'), Law No 434 of 20 June 1989, as amended by Law No 308 of 16 May, 1990 (effective from 1 April 1991).

These statutes cover all aspects of public/private company legislation, apart from tax legislation and accounts legislation. (Some rules may also be found in certain other specific legislation such as the Environmental Protection Act.)

Private companies

Private companies are subject to the Danish Private Companies Act ('anpartsselskabsloven'), Law Announcement No 7 of 13 January 1984, as amended by Law No. 286 of 6 June 1984, Law No. 53 of 20 February 1985, and Law No.308 of 16 May, 1990 (effective from 1 April 1991). Other legislation (apart from tax legislation) includes the Act on Annual Accounts, Law Announcement No 436 of 20 June 20 1989.

What are the requirements for the management structure of these companies?

Public companies
A public company must have a 'bestyrelse' ('board of directors') and a 'direktion' ('board of managers'). A member of the board of directors will be referred to as a 'director'. A member of the board of managers is referred to as a 'manager'.

The board of directors is headed by a 'formand' ('chairperson') and the board of directors appoints the board of managers consisting of one to three members (or more).

The board of directors and the board of managers are jointly in charge of the overall management of the company. As a consequence, the management normally participates in the meetings of the board of directors, but without voting rights.

The board of directors also has a supervisory function in relation to the management and is broadly responsible for the orderly organisation of the company. The board also ensures that the book-keeping and the administration of the assets of the company are controlled in a satisfactory way.

The board of managers is in charge of the day-to-day management of the company and must follow the directions and guidelines set out by the board of directors.

Private Companies
The position, as described above in relation to public companies also applies to private companies, with a share capital of more than 300,000 Dkr with more than 50 employees. However, if the private company's capital is less than 300,000 Dkr and it has less than 50 employees, then it does not need to have a board of directors at all, or it may appoint a board of directors with fewer than three members.

If the private company does not have a board of directors, then the board of managers (which may consist of only one person) is elected at the shareholders' meeting and carries out the duties both of the board of directors and of the board of managers.

If private companies do have a board of directors, then the rules mentioned under public companies apply.

How many directors must a Danish company have?

Public companies
Public companies must have a board of directors consisting of at least three members, but there is no upper limit. The company's articles of association, which define the powers of the company and the way it conducts its

business, also state the number of board members. Although there is no legal obligation to appoint deputies for the directors elected at the shareholders' meeting, if deputies are appointed, then the rules applicable to directors apply to them also.

Private companies
In private companies with a capital of less than 300,000 Dkr and fewer than 50 employees, as there is no requirement for a minimum number of directors, the articles of association may state that the board of directors can consist of fewer than three members or indeed may provide that the company has no board of directors at all, and can be run by a single executive.

If the company's capital exceeds 300,000 Dkr, a board of directors consisting of at least three members must be appointed.

There is no requirement to appoint deputies for directors elected at the shareholders' meeting but, if they are, they are under the same obligations as other board members.

Are there any requirements for employee representation?
The employees in both public and private companies, which have over the last three years employed on average at least 35 persons (which includes employed persons aged 15 years or more, excluding the board of managers and employees who work permanently outside Denmark), have a right to appoint a number of directors and deputies from among the employees. These appointees are in addition to the ones appointed by the shareholders. This number may correspond to up to half of the board members appointed at the shareholders' meeting, who in any event can appoint at least two directors.

If a parent company has subsidiary companies registered in Denmark and the parent company has a majority of votes in the subsidiary company, and between them the companies have over the last three years employed on average at least 35 employees, the employees have the right to elect a number of members of the board of directors of the parent company. (If the subsidiary company itself employs more than 35 persons on average over the last three years, the rule outlined in the paragraph above will apply separately to the subsidiary.)

Even if a company does not fall within the above provisions, the articles of association may provide that the employees of the company or group, as the case may be, shall have the right to elect two or more members of the board of directors.

The election among the employees takes place before the annual shareholders' meeting.

Who appoints a director?

Public companies

The board of directors (excluding those appointed by the employees) is usually elected by the shareholders at the shareholders' meeting. However, the articles of association may provide for election of board members by a shareholders' committee, elected at the shareholders' meeting. The articles of association can also authorise third parties to appoint one or more directors. The majority of directors must in any case be elected at the shareholders' meeting (unless they are elected by the shareholders' committee). Agreements among the shareholders concerning the election of directors can also be made. Although such agreements can be made orally, because of the problem of enforcement, any such agreement would normally be in writing.

The employee representatives are elected by the employees from among eligible employees. These are employees who have full legal capacity and have been employed by the company (or group) for the preceding 12 months. A resolution to admit persons elected by the employees as members of the board of directors must be passed by not less than half of the company's employees.

Private companies

If the private company has a board of directors, then the board is elected at the shareholders' meeting. If the company only has a manager, he or she is appointed at the shareholders' meeting. A private company may have a shareholders' committee, but in practice this would be very unusual.

Where employee representatives are elected on to the board of a private company, the same rules as those applicable to public companies apply.

Is there any limitation on the number of directorships which an individual can hold in public and private companies?

No. An individual may hold any number of directorships either in a personal capacity or as a representative of another company.

Who can be a director?

Public and private companies

- The majority of the members of the board of directors must be persons who are not managers of the company.

- The directors and the managers of the company must have full legal capacity, ie they must be at least 18 years old and must not be incapacitated.
- Managers and not less than half of the members of the board of directors must be residents of Denmark, unless the Minister of Industry grants exemption from this provision. According to Executive Order No 489 of 4 July 1989, EC citizens are generally granted exemption from this provision. Additionally, Scandinavian citizens are usually granted exemption.
- The manager of the company cannot be elected as chairman of the board of directors.
- In companies whose object is to carry on shipping, a one-man business or a general partnership may be appointed manager, provided the proprietor or the partners meet the above-mentioned requirements.
- Apart from the above rules in the Public Companies Act and the Private Companies Act, other Acts set out further requirements in relation to directors in certain specific circumstances. For example, according to the Danish Maritime Act at least two-thirds of the board of directors in a company which owns a ship sailing under the Danish flag must be Danish citizens and resident in Denmark.
- In addition, the board of directors or the articles of association may lay down further procedural rules or requirements as to who may become a director, for example, that they must be less than 70 years of age or that they must be shareholders.
- Employee representatives are elected, for a period of four years at a time, from among employees who have been employed for at least one year immediately preceding the election. These directors are subject to the same procedural rules as to age, duty and capacity as other directors and can be reappointed at the end of the four-year period.

Who is excluded from being a director?

Public and private companies

- People who do not fulfil the above-mentioned requirements may not become directors of companies.
- State authorised public accountants are prevented from simultaneously being a director or a manager or an employee of a company of an institution which engages in any business other than auditing. The Danish Commerce and Companies Agency may grant exemption from this rule if it is considered that the company has no influence on the accountant's position as an independent accountant.

- Bank managers are excluded by law from being directors.
- As a matter of practice, ministers, judges and higher government officials are also generally excluded from being directors.

What is the relationship between a company and the directors?

Public companies
The directors do not have to be shareholders in the company. A director of the company is not necessarily an employee, but he or she may have a service contract with the company. The employee representatives retain their employee status and continue their normal working duties for the company, independently of their duties as directors.

Private companies
The board of directors and/or the managers of the company are usually shareholders of the company, although this is not a requirement. As for the employees, the same rules as mentioned above under public companies are applicable.

How is a director rewarded?

In both public and private companies, directors may be paid a fixed salary and/or a bonus which must be calculated as a percentage of the year's profits. However, if the board of directors is to receive the right to a bonus, this must be provided for in the articles of association. It is sufficient to state in the articles of association that the percentage of the bonus can be established each year at the shareholders' meeting. The amount paid to the directors appears in the annual accounts. These accounts are available for inspection by the public.

Managers are usually treated in the same way as employees.

Are there any restrictions on benefits which the directors can receive from the company?

Public and private companies
Yes. Apart from the above restriction as to the need for the articles to provide for the right to a bonus, Article 115, Public Companies Act and Article 84, Private Companies Act state that a company may not grant, loan to or provide security for shareholders, directors or managers of the company or its parent company or to/for any of the above mentioned persons' relatives in any personal capacity.

What are the tax and social security contributions to be paid by a director?

Public and private companies
If the director is remunerated for his work as a director the salary, and/or the bonus, is subject to normal income tax, but is not subject to social security contributions and consequently there are no corresponding social security benefits. A manager's salary is subject to normal income tax and also to social security contributions with corresponding benefits.

What is the basis of a director's authority?

Public and Private Companies
A director's authority is derived from four sources:

- Statutes, ie the Danish Public Companies Act and the Danish Private Companies Act.
- The articles of association.
- The rules of procedure for the board of directors which are set out as the board may direct. Normally, the rules are in a fairly standard form, but individual rules may be added. The law does not give directions as to what the rules of procedure must contain.
- Shareholders' decisions, other agreements and any other special rules, for example the Bank and Savings Bank Act which includes special rules for directors of banks, and the Environmental Protection Act which states, for example, that a director or manager may be personally liable for environmental damage caused by a company.

What are the powers of a director?

Public companies
To manage the affairs of the company Article 54, Public Companies Act states that the board of directors and the board of managers are in charge of the management of the company's affairs. The board of directors is responsible for the overall policy and (justifiable) organisation of the company and it is the board of directors which has the power to appoint the management of the company. The managers are responsible for the day-to-day management of the company and must follow the rules and instructions set out by the board of directors.
To authorise significant disposals The day-to-day management does not include disposals which are unusual or of great importance for the company. Such disposals can only be made by the management if they have special permission from the board of directors. The only limited exception

to this rule is where delay in obtaining such permission would be against the interests of the company. In this case, the board of directors must be informed as soon as possible of the dispositions made by the management.

To control administration The board of directors must ensure that the book-keeping and the administration of property is controlled in a satisfactory way.

To represent the company Article 60 states that the directors and managers represent the company. A company is bound by contracts entered into on its behalf by the members of the board of directors, jointly or by one of its members, or by a manager.

Article 61 further provides that a contract entered into on behalf of a company by a person to whom the power to bind the company has been conferred binds the company, unless the persons who have power to bind the company have acted outside the restrictions imposed on their powers by the Act, or the contract is outside the objects of the company and the company proves that the third party is, or should have been, aware of this. The articles of companies are registered with a Registrar of Companies, and are available for public inspection.

To increase the share capital The articles of association may state that a board of directors in a public company may increase the share capital of the company. This authorisation is limited to a period not in excess of five years at any one time. The articles of association must state the date on which the authorisation will terminate and the highest amount to which the board of directors may increase the company's capital. The five-year period only relates to the granting of the power. (The board of directors has no power to reduce the share capital nor may the articles of association authorise the directors to make such a decision. Only the shareholders in general meeting can decide to reduce the share capital.)

Private companies

The rules relating to the powers of directors of a private company are substantially the same.

Article 36 corresponds to the provisions of Article 54, Public Companies Act, while Articles 41 and 42 correspond to Articles 60 and 61, Public Companies Act respectively.

The board of directors in a private company has the power to appoint the management of the company.

How are the powers of a director restricted?

Public and private companies

Special interest There is a special interest restriction which provides that a director or a manager of the company may not participate in any of the following transactions or matters if such director or manager has any material interest therein which may be contrary to that of the interests of the company:

- contracts between the company and such director or manager;
- legal actions against the director or manager by the company;
- contracts between the company and any third party; or legal actions against any third party.

By the articles The articles of association may provide that the power to bind the company, which under the Public Companies Act and the Private Companies Act is conferred on the individual members of the board of directors and managers, shall be restricted so that such power shall only be exercised by several members jointly or by one or more named members individually or jointly. No other restrictions on the power to bind the company may be included or are able to be registered.

Undue advantage No persons authorised to represent the company may act in such a way as to enable certain shareholders or others to obtain an undue advantage at the expense of other shareholders of the company. Nor may any such authorised person put into effect resolutions passed by the company in general meeting or by other company bodies if such resolutions are contrary to the relevant Acts or the articles of association.

The objects of the company The board of directors must act within the objects of the company. Note, however, Article 61, Public Companies Act and its equivalent Article 42, Private Companies Act mentioned above.

Other authorities The directors must respect the authority given to other bodies within the company, such as the shareholders in general meeting who have, for example, authority regarding the following:

- modification of the articles of association;
- approval of the annual accounts and the allocation of profits or the covering of losses according to the adopted accounts;
- approval of an acquisition by the company of the assets of a shareholder;
- the appointment of directors;
- the appointment of auditors.

Other restrictions The powers of a director may be subject to further restrictions in the articles of association or in other relevant agreements between the shareholders.

What are the duties of a director?

Public and private companies

Only the most important duties of a director under the Public Companies Act and the Private Companies Act are listed below.

- In a public company, the board of directors must ensure a) that the company is a going concern and b) that the book-keeping and the administration of the assets of the company are being properly controlled and administered.

  With regard to private companies, although these rules are not set out in the Private Companies Act, in fact the board of directors of private companies is also responsible for its actions. As a part of this duty for both public and private companies, the board must appoint and maintain a board of managers.

- In both public and private companies, the board of directors must, under the rules of procedure as set out by the board of directors itself, lay down further provisions as to the duties and powers of directors ('forretningsorden').

  — In public companies, should the company lose half its subscribed share capital, then the board must call and hold a meeting of shareholders within six months of that loss. At the shareholders' meeting, the board of directors must give an account of the financial position of the company and must submit proposals for arrangements such as the dissolution of the company.

  — Should this happen in a private company, the board of directors must submit proposals that will restore in full the subscribed capital or a proposal for the dissolution of the company. A shareholders' meeting must also be called within the six-month period.

- The board of directors convenes the shareholders' meetings. There must be at least one annual shareholders' meeting for the presenting of the annual accounts. Apart from this, a shareholders' meeting may be held whenever necessary (eg to elect a new board member in the middle of the year if someone resigns).

- The board of directors presents the annual accounts and the proposal as to dividends at the annual shareholders' meeting.

- On the demand of a shareholder, provided that in the opinion of the board it may be done without any serious harmful effects for the company, the board of directors and the managers must at the shareholders' meeting give all available information concerning:

— matters of importance to enable the proper evaluation of the annual accounts, the annual report and the group accounts (if any);

— the state of affairs of the company in all other cases; or

— questions to be decided upon by the company in general meeting.

● There is also a duty to employees under employment legislation.

The last four sections apply to both public and private companies.

How does the board of directors operate internally?

Public and private companies
The board of directors elects its own chairperson in the absence of any provision to the contrary in the articles of association. In the case of a parity of votes, such election shall be decided by drawing lots. A manager of the company (registered as such in the Commerce and Companies Agency) may not be elected chairperson. The chairperson arranges for the board of directors to hold meetings whenever necessary, and ensures that all directors are given due notice of the meeting.

May any director or manager request a meeting?

Yes. Any director or a manager may at any time request that a meeting of the directors be called and, even if a manager is not a member of the board of directors, he or she is entitled to attend and to speak at meetings of directors, unless the directors decide otherwise at any time.

Are records of meetings kept?

Yes. Proceedings of directors' meetings are recorded in a minute book which must be signed by all directors attending. A director or manager not agreeing to a resolution passed by the board is entitled to have his or her opinion entered into the minute book. It should be noted that resolutions can be passed in writing without the need for the directors to meet.

Are there any further provisions as to duties and powers of directors?

Yes. The board of directors must, by rules of procedure, lay down further provisions as to the duties and powers of directors. The law gives no further directions as to what the rules of procedure must contain. A quorum is deemed to exist when more than half of all the directors attend the meeting, unless the articles of association provide for a higher number. Resolutions may not be passed, however, unless all directors have, as far as possible, been given an opportunity to participate in the relevant discussion. If a deputy has been elected for an absent director, such deputy has the right to deputise for such director in his or her absence at any future meetings, provided the said director remains absent. The business transacted by the board of directors shall, unless the articles of association require a special majority of votes, be decided by a simple majority of votes. The articles of association may provide that in the case of a parity of votes the chairperson shall be given a casting vote.

What are the penalties for a breach of duty by main board directors?

Directors who have, in the performance of their duties, intentionally or negligently caused loss or harm to the company, are liable to pay compensation for such loss or harm. The same applies when such loss or harm has been inflicted on shareholders, creditors of the company or third parties by violation of the duties under the Acts or the articles of association. This rule corresponds to the normal damages rule according to Danish law – the 'culpa rule'.

The board members may be liable individually or collectively.

The director may, of course, also be liable under the Danish Criminal Act, for example in cases of fraud, theft from the company etc. In certain cases, directors in breach of directors' duties (for example, breach of the statutory duties relating to the filing of accounts) may be fined under the Public/Private Companies Act.

Is a company liable for the default of its director?

In both public and private companies, as mentioned above, a contract entered into on behalf of the company by a person on whom the power to bind the company has been conferred binds the company, unless:

- the persons who have power to bind the company have acted in contravention of the restrictions imposed on their powers by the Public Companies Act or the Private Companies Act; or
- the contract is outside the objects of the company, and the company proves that the third party had or ought to have had notice of the fact.

In all other cases the company is liable, even though there is a default by one of its directors but, in this case, the company can take civil proceedings against the director for damages under Article 140 Public Companies Act or Article 110, Private Companies Act.

In cases where the company infringes environmental regulations for example, the company may be fined and the directors may additionally have independent liability under the relevant legislation.

The company as a legal entity does not face criminal liability. Instead, those authorised to represent the company may be subject to criminal liability as mentioned above.

What are the accounting responsibilities?

The law in relation to the presentation of accounts is set out in the Act on Annual Accounts, Law Announcement No 436 of 20 June 1989. Its main provisions are described briefly below.

Article 2

Each accounting year (which does not have to follow the calendar year) the board of directors and the board of managers prepare an annual account in accordance with statute and the articles of association, together with an annual report. In parent companies, a group company account must also be prepared.

The account must be available at least eight days before the annual shareholders' meeting at which the account is presented by the board of directors. The account must bear the auditor's attestation.

The account must be signed by the board of directors and the board of managers. If one of these persons cannot accept the accounts, his or her objection must be recorded in the accounts.

Article 3

The account must relate to a 12-month period. A company's first accounting period may comprise a shorter or longer period than 12 months, but the maximum period allowable is 18 months.

Each company in a group must have the same accounting year, unless some special reason is given to the contrary.

Articles 4–55

These Articles set out the rules for the making and the setting up of the accounts.

Article 56

The annual report must give an accurate and truthful account of the company's activities and situation, and this Article sets out the details which the annual report must contain. These are:

- if the annual account is affected by an unusual situation or if there is some uncertainty concerning the establishment of the accounting information, this must be specified;
- important events which have occurred since the termination of the latest accounting year;
- the future trends or general plans of the company;
- Research and development activity;

- a proposal from the board of directors as to dividends or the covering of losses.

Articles 57–61
These establish the rules for the preparation of the annual accounts of a group company.

Articles 61a–61l
These establish the rules for the company's state authorised public accountants.

Articles 62–64b
These establish the rules for the publication of the accounts, ie no later than one month after the annual accounts have been adopted at the shareholders' meeting, and not later than seven months after the end of the accounting period, a copy of the revised annual accounts and the annual report must be sent to the Commerce and Companies Agency. Companies coming within Article 55 do not have to send the annual report to the Commerce and Companies Agency, but they are required to disclose additional information (eg the names and addresses of all shareholders holding at least 5 per cent of the total voting rights) in the annual accounts. A company comes within Article 55 if, at the date of the balance (normally the last day of the accounting year), it does not exceed two of the following three sizes:

- a balance of 12 million Dkr;
- a net sale of 24 million Dkr and
- an average of 50 full-time employees during the accounting year.

If the company is a group company, each of the companies or the group as a whole must not exceed two of the three sizes mentioned above if it is to come within Article 55.

Article 65
Wilful or serious breach of (*inter alia*) Article 2, s1, Articles 3–9, 56–9, 52, and s1–3 Article 62 can result in fines being imposed.

What are the consequences of a company insolvency for the directors?
The consequences in both private and public companies' insolvencies for directors are:

- as to the duties of a director to take action if half of the share capital is lost. (see above);
- if a company continues to trade after it is insolvent then the board of

directors or a single director can be liable in accordance with the above-mentioned rules for losses suffered by a shareholder which are caused by the continuation;

- when winding-up proceedings are brought against a company, the board of directors of the company is replaced by a liquidator or a trustee. The liquidator or the trustee takes over all responsibilities of the board of directors, and he or she is the only person who can enter into contracts on behalf of the company.

How does an individual cease to be a director?

In both public and private companies a director can cease to be a board member for the following reasons.

- When his or her term of office as a director ends. In practice, a board member is normally elected for one year at a time and then re-elected every year at the annual shareholders' meeting. However, the duration is generally fixed in the articles of association, although in any event a director's initial (and any subsequent) term of office may not exceed four years. The directors appointed by the employees are appointed for four years at a time.
- When the company itself ceases to operate, or winding-up proceedings are brought against the company and a liquidator or a trustee is appointed.
- If the director is removed from his or her position. A member of the board of directors may be removed at any time by the body that elected or nominated him or her (normally this will be the shareholders).
- If the director resigns. A member of the board of directors may resign from the board at any time. Notice of such resignation must be given to the board of directors and, when the member has not been elected at the shareholders' meeting, also to the body which nominated him or her.
- A board member elected by the employees from among the employees ceases to be a director when he or she is no longer employed by the company.
- If the director ceases to be eligible as a member of the board of directors, for example because he or she no longer has full legal capacity, because he or she no longer resides in Denmark, or because more than half the members of the board are no longer resident in Denmark and the Minister of Industry does not grant exemption from this provision, and the standard exemptions do not apply.
- Retirement due to age as may be stated in the articles of association.

Where a member of the board of directors retires from his or her office before the expiration of his or her term of office, or where he or she is no longer qualified to be a member of the board of directors and where there is no deputy to replace him, the other members of the board of directors are responsible for organising the election of a new member to hold office for the remaining term of office of the retiring member. This provision also applies if the member of the board of directors elected by the employees is no longer employed by the company or the group. When the member is to be elected at the shareholders' meeting, the election of a new member for the board of directors may, however, be postponed to the next ordinary shareholders' meeting when election of directors is to take place, provided always that the board of directors can form a quorum with the remaining directors and deputies.

Do the above-mentioned rules apply as well to a shadow director?

The concept of a 'shadow director' as such is not known in Danish companies. However, a major shareholder may be bound by certain statutory rules which state that the rights of minor shareholders have to be respected in some matters. In addition, a major shareholder may be liable for any damage he or she causes to the company or other shareholders, but this arises from his or her position as shareholder and not through the concept of being a 'shadow director'.

How has the insider dealing directive been implemented in the Public Companies Act and the Private Companies Act?

Public companies
According to Article 53, Public Companies Act, the individual members of the board of directors (including deputies) and the management of a company must, when taking up their posts as members of the board of directors or the management, inform the board of directors of their holdings of shares in companies and private companies within the same group, and they must give notice of their acquisition and sale of such shares. Such notice is recorded in a special register. In the case of group companies, the board of directors may decide to keep a register common to all the companies in the group.

Directors and managers must not embark upon or participate in any speculative transactions relating to shares in the company or relating to shares in companies within the same group. This applies whenever they may have price-sensitive information or buy or sell to influence the price (the 'principle of demand') thereby obtaining a financial gain.

Private companies
The same rule appears in Article 35, Private Companies Act.

Public and private companies
If a director or a manager of either a public or a private company violates these rules, he or she may be fined.

For public companies registered on the Stock Exchange, Article 39, Stock Exchange Act applies. This rule states that no one who is in possession of unpublished information concerning the company or its shares may trade in such stocks if the information may influence the price of the shares. Article 31 states that directors, managers and other employees in a stockbroking company may not unlawfully reveal any information they have received in the course of their work or while carrying out duties for the company.

In 1987 the board of the Copenhagen Stock Exchange adopted the 'Stock Exchange Rules of Ethics'. Article 7 states that 'Any attempt to influence pricing through dishonest means constitutes a violation of the Stock Exchange Rules of Ethics'.

The board of directors, management, other executives and shareholders must abstain from any action which may prove detrimental to the normal and honest trade of the company shares and/or may prove detrimental to investors, or may give certain shareholders an undue benefit at the expense of other shareholders or the company.

Nobody who in his or her professional capacity has obtained information on dealing, or other information concerning companies listed on the Stock Exchange, may use such information for the purpose of influencing the market artificially.

The board of the Copenhagen Stock Exchange also recommends that companies registered on the Stock Exchange conform to the following rule:

> The board of directors, managers and other executives, who have been so instructed by the board of directors, may only buy and sell their shares in the company within six weeks after the publication of the annual and semi-annual reports, quarterly or other section reports concerning the accounts. The sale of shares outside these periods may take place in special cases after notification of the chairman of the board.

What is the scope of product liability in Denmark and who is responsible for it?
Product liability is the term which refers to the liability imposed on the

manufacturer, distributor or seller of a defective product for the damage caused by the defective product, either to a person or to someone's property. The Product Liability Act No 371 of 7 June 1989 is a consumer protection Act.

A manufacturer, distributor or seller of such a defective product can be held liable to pay damages under the Product Liability Act. According to this Act, an injured party can recover damages according to the rules which existed before the Act, or according to the rules stated in the Act:

1. Under the rules which existed before the Act, an injured party can recover damages unless the supplier can prove that the damage was not his or her fault.

2. The rules in the Product Liability Act establish strict liability for the manufacturer and the supplier, ie the injured party can recover damages for financial loss and/or personal injury from the manufacturer or the supplier, even though they are not at fault. (There are a few exceptions to this rule.) There is no maximum limit on the amount of damages which may be recoverable.

In non-consumer cases, the injured party may only recover damages in accordance with 1, above.

A director is not generally liable for the defective products of his or her company, and, therefore, does not have to compensate the injured persons or pay damages, unless for some reason he or she has an independent liability because he or she has been in breach of his or her duties as director, as described above.

FRANCE

Christian Belloin, Brigitte Lindner

What are the main types of company which exist in France?
There are two forms of company in France, a public company and a private company:

- a 'Société Anonyme' (which can be recognised by the letters 'SA' after the name of the company) is the public company form, and is the structure used by large enterprises requiring a large capital base;
- a 'Société à Responsabilité Limitée' (which can be recognised by the letters 'Sàrl') is the private company form and the structure usually chosen by smaller businesses.

What is a Eurl (Enterprise Unipersonnelle à Responsabilité Limitée)?
It is possible for a Sàrl to have only one shareholder and it is then called an 'Entreprise Unipersonnelle à Responsabilité Limitée' (Eurl). The single shareholder of an Eurl can be either a 'real' or a corporate person, including another Eurl. However, a real person can be the sole shareholder of only one Eurl, and a Eurl itself can be the sole shareholder of only one other Eurl.

What about French company legislation?
The company legislation is mainly set out in two Acts:

- the 'Loi No.66–537 du 24 juillet 1966' (1966 Act);
- 'Decret No.67–236 du 23 mars 1967' (1967 Decree).

MANAGEMENT OF AN SA

What are the requirements for the management structure of an SA?
An SA can be managed in one of two ways.

- The SA may have a 'Conseil d'administration'. For translation purposes this is hereinafter referred to as a 'board of directors'. Responsible for the management of the company, it is headed by a 'Président Directeur Général' (PDG), the equivalent of a Chairperson. The PDG is the president of the board and is responsible for representing the company to third parties. The PDG may be assisted by one, two or five Directeurs Généraux (DG) depending on the amount of the share capital.

- Alternatively the company may have a form of management split between two different boards, (a) the so called 'directoire', which is an executive board and (b) the 'Consent de Surveillance', a supervisory board. This system has German law as its inspiration but it should be carefully distinguished from the management of a German AG by a 'Vorstand' and 'Aufsichtsrat'. The executive board manages the company on a day-to-day basis.

The 'Président du Directoire' is responsible for representing the company, with regard to third persons, although each member of the directorate has wide powers to act in the name of the company. The articles of association may empower the supervisory board to provide one or more other members of the directorate with the company's representation. They are then called 'Directeur général'.

This executive board is controlled by a supervisory board, the 'Conseil de surveillance', whose members are appointed by the shareholders' meeting. The supervisory board is not concerned with the general management of the company, but rather with the control of the management of the company. Control of the company's management means that at any stage of the financial year the supervisory board may control the running of the business as carried out by the members of the executive board. The control includes the grant of authorisations for special transactions. The supervisory board is further involved in the appointment of the members of the executive board. As the supervisory board is not involved in the management of the company itself it will only be considered in so far as it affects the control of the executive board.

Which of the two management structures is the most usual?

The single tier board, the 'Conseil d'administration', is by far the more popular management format and in fact the two tier executive and supervisory board system is rather unusual.

How many directors does a company have?

The number of directors of a 'Conseil d'administration' is fixed by the articles of association within the statutory limitations (minimum: 3; maximum: 12). For companies listed on the Stock Exchange, the minimum is 3 and the maximum is 15.

If a two tier system applies, the number of members of the executive board is either fixed by the articles of association or by the supervisory board. The executive board cannot have more than five members, unless it is a company listed on the Stock Exchange, in which case it may have seven members. If the company's share capital exceeds 1 million FFr, the executive board must have at least two members.

How many members must a supervisory board have?

The supervisory board must have at least three members and not more than 12. The articles of association usually fix the number of members of the supervisory board within the limits provided for by statute.

Are there any requirements for employee representation?

Companies may be required to have a Workers' Representation Committee (ie companies with more than 50 employees or companies with less than 50 employees if such establishment is required by a collective bargaining agreement), and in such cases two representatives of that committee have the right to attend each meeting of the board of directors or supervisory board of the company. At such meetings, the representatives may express the opinion of the Workers Representation Committee which is based upon the opinion of the employees.

Secondly, any company's articles may state that employees should have some board positions.

Further, the representation of employees on the board of directors ('Conseil d'Administration') is a statutory requirement where an SA has at least 200 employees and the French Government has owned at least 50 per cent of the shares for at least six months. The employee board members must be elected by the employees, and the number will be fixed by the articles of association. The statutory maximum is four and the employees must not constitute more than one third of all the board members.

Who can be a director?

By law, members of the board of directors ('Conseil d'Administration') of an SA must be shareholders of the SA. If they are not shareholders on their appointment, they must become shareholders within three months. The number of shares the directors must have will be determined by the articles of association and must not be less than the number of shares needed for shareholders to participate in a shareholders' general meeting as provided for by the articles of association. However, this does not apply to members of the executive board who need not be shareholders.

It is possible for a company to be a member of the board of directors of another company. If this occurs, then the director company must appoint a person as its permanent representative.

Who can be a président directeur general (PDG) of a company?

By law a PDG must be a member of the board, an individual (and not corporate) person, not over (generally) 65 years of age (although the articles of association may provide a lower or higher age limit). No one may be a PDG of more than two companies.

Who can be a directeur général?

A DG must be an individual and not a corporate person, not over 65 years old, unless otherwise provided in the articles of association. It is not compulsory for a DG to be a member of the board of directors or a shareholder in the company and there is no limit to the number of companies for which a person can be a DG.

Who is excluded from being a director?

The following people cannot be directors:

- legally incapacitated persons;
- members of parliament (for some companies);
- civil servants (for some companies);
- auditors of the company or someone who has been an auditor of the company in the preceding five years.
- an individual cannot be a director of more than eight companies. However, there are certain exceptions to this rule, the most important being that an individual who is a director of eight companies can be a director of a further five companies if at least 20 per cent of each of those companies' capital is owned by companies in which they are already directors. This rule does not apply to those people who sit on boards as the representatives of a company which is a director itself;
- age limit – one-third of the directors cannot be older than 70, unless the articles of association provide otherwise.

May foreign nationals be members of the board?

Nationals of foreign countries can be members of boards of directors, executive boards or supervisory boards. However, nationals of countries which are not members of the European Community must apply for a 'Carte de Commerçant' if they want to be a PDG, DG or a member of the executive board of an SA. However, foreign members of a supervisory board do not need any commercial card.

Who appoints the members of the board of directors?

- On the formation of an SA with a public offer of shares, the directors will be elected at the initial shareholder meeting.

- If the SA does not make a public share offer the directors will be appointed through the articles.
- At all other times the directors will be appointed by the shareholders in any general meeting.

Who elects the employee representatives?
The employee representative directors are elected by those employees who have been employed for at least three months.

Who appoints the PDG and the DG?
The PDG and the DG are appointed by the board of directors.

Who appoints the members of an executive board?
The members of the executive board and its chairperson are appointed by the supervisory board.

Who appoints the supervisory board?
As in the case of a director, the members of the supervisory board are appointed at the initial shareholders' meeting, if the SA makes a public offer of shares. If this is not the case, then the members of the supervisory board are appointed by the articles of association. At all other times, the members of the supervisory board are appointed by the shareholders in any general meeting.

What is the relationship between a company and a director?
As a general rule the officers of a company are not considered to be employees. They have a special role within the company defined by the law as a 'mandate'.

The general rule is that a director cannot also be employed by the company, but there are exceptions to this rule.

What about an employee who becomes a director of a board of directors?
If an employee becomes a director, his or her employment contract will only remain valid if the following conditions apply:

- the employee has had an employment contract with the company for at least two years (unless the company has been established for less than two years);
- the contract must be a legally binding document, be duly executed and be effective;
- less than one-third of the directors have an employment contract.

If the employee has been employed for less than two years, the employment contract is no longer valid once the employee becomes a director. There is some debate as to whether or not it is possible to suspend the contract for the duration of the directorship. Recent case-law has established that such a suspension is possible.

Does this also apply to members of an executive board?
The members of an executive board can have a service agreement with the company. If such a contract is agreed after the appointment of the director, then special provisions for contracts concluded between the company and one of its directors will apply.

What about members of the supervisory board?
It is not possible for a member of the supervisory board to have a service agreement with the company.

How are the members of a board of directors rewarded?
The members of the board of directors of an SA receive a special payment called 'Jetons de Présence' for their attendance at board meetings (an attendance fee for the time passed in the meeting). If the members of the board have a valid service agreement they may also receive a salary; payment for any expenses they have legitimately incurred for the benefit of the company may also be paid.

Any other payments, especially any form of profit-sharing to the members of the board of directors, are strictly prohibited.

The amount of the 'Jetons de Présence' is decided by the shareholders in general meeting. The amount they fix is the total figure of 'Jetons de Présence' for the whole board. The board of directors then divides this amount between its members at its discretion.

What about the rewards of a PDG?
The PDG may receive 'Jetons de Présence' for his or her role as a director and also a special remuneration for his or her role as a PDG. This amount may be a fixed sum, an amount proportional to the company's turnover or profits, or a combination of the two which will be decided by the board.

Who decides about the remuneration of a DG?
The remuneration of a DG is fixed by the board of directors.

Are there any restrictions on benefits which a director can receive from the company?
Under s106 of the Act concerning law no. 66–537 (July 1966), there is a total prohibition against a company conferring any loan, granting any

overdraft protection or giving any other form of security to a director of the company.

Where a company is a director, this prohibition extends to the permanent representatives on the board of the company.

What tax contributions must be paid by a director?

- The attendance fees ('Jetons de Présence') of directors of an SA who are not at the same time employees of a French company are taxed in the security income category.
- Special compensation paid to directors for particular tasks is taxed as salary.
- The compensation paid to PDG, DG and members of the directorate is also taxed as salary. However, the compensation paid to the president and vice president of the supervisory board is taxed in the security income category.

What about social security contributions?

Directors of an SA who receive only 'Jetons de Présence' are not obliged to make social security contributions. If they also have a service contract, these 'Jetons de Présence' are not taken into account for the amount of social security contributions to be paid.

The PDG and the DG, as well as the members of the directorate who receive a special remuneration for their service to the company, are obliged to contribute to the social security plan and are entitled to get benefits.

What is the basis of a director's authority?

The authority of a director is derived from three sources:

- statute, ie the 1966 Act and the 1967 Decree;
- the articles of association;
- shareholders' decisions as well as decisions of the board of directors.

What are the powers of a director?

Section 98 of the 1966 Act gives the board of directors the power to act in the name of the company. The members of the board must act collectively. The 1966 Act sets out the various powers and duties of directors collectively, such as:

- the ability to call a general meeting of the shareholders;
- the duty to prepare the annual reports and accounts;

- the ability to authorise contracts made between the company and one of the members of the board of directors or DGs;
- the ability to appoint a director when necessary;
- the ability to appoint and dismiss the PDG and DG and the ability to set the amount of their remuneration;
- the power to allocate among the directors the 'Jetons de Présence';
- the ability to confirm the increase of the company's share capital when convertible debentures are converted;
- the ability to transfer the company's registered office within the 'département' (county) with the approval of the shareholders;
- the ability to authorise a guarantee made by the company and given to a third party.

There are no individual powers of the members of the 'Conseil d' Administration', except the right to get individual information which will put the director in a position to judge the situation of the company's affairs himself.

What about the powers of a PDG?

The PDG has the widest powers to act in the name of the company. His main powers are set out in s 113 of the 1966 Act. The PDG has wide general management powers and the ability to represent the company in negotiations and dealings with third parties.

The power of a DG is decided on by the board of directors and the PDG. This power can be as wide as the power of the company PDG.

What are the powers of the executive board?

The members of the executive board ('directoire') have identical powers to those of a PDG, i.e. they manage and represent the company *vis-à-vis* third parties and deal with the day-to-day business of the company (s L124 of the 1966 Act).

The members of the executive board must act collectively unless the supervisory board authorises a division of the management tasks between several members of the directorate (provided that this method of management is not prohibited by the articles).

The company is represented by the president of the 'Directoire' or a general director (DG).

In the case of a conflict between the executive board and the supervisory board, the supervisory board may call a general shareholders' meeting for the dismissal of a member of the directorate.

The executive board is required to do the following:

- submit quarterly reports to the supervisory board detailing the curr
  situation of the company;
- prepare the annual accounts and annual report;
- submit documents showing the current strategy of the company.

How are the powers of a member of the board of directors restricted?

A director's powers are restricted by the 1966 Act, but may be subject to further restrictions in the articles of association. When an SA has an executive board this is controlled by a supervisory board.

The following restrictions on the board of directors should be noted:

- they must act within the objects of the company;
- the directors must respect the other areas of authority within the company, such as the shareholders in general meeting.
- another restriction on the power of directors is set out in ss 101–3 of the 1966 Act and comes from the basic principle of conflict of interest. The authorisation of the board of directors must be obtained by the directors and/or DG if they propose that the company enters directly or indirectly into a contract with a director and/or DG on a matter which does not relate to the normal business of the company and which is not concluded upon the 'normal terms'. The director him or herself must submit details to the board of the proposed contract prior to its execution. This must then be put before the shareholders in general meeting for their approval to be decided by a simple majority. It is not possible for a director to contract a loan directly from the company, unless the company is a bank.

How are the powers of a PDG restricted?

The powers of a PDG are restricted in the same way as the powers of directors. In addition to this, a PDG's authority may be limited by the board of directors. According to the Act, a PDG is not allowed to give guarantees to third parties without the prior approval of the board of directors. These rules also apply to a DG.

How are the powers of an executive board restricted?

When an SA is managed by an executive board the powers of the directors are restricted to acting within the objects of the company and any decisions made by the shareholders in general meeting. Apart from this the executive board is subject to the control of the supervisory board.

53

What does control of the executive board by the supervisory board mean?

- First of all the supervisory board has the permanent control of the executive board. In order to exercise this control the supervisory board receives quarterly reports from the executive board and may examine the books and records of the company at any stage.
- The supervisory board alone has the power to authorise certain matters such as the giving of guarantees, and the sale and purchase of land.
- Other special powers of the supervisory board are:

    — the power to appoint the members of the executive board and determine their level of remuneration;
    — the power to appoint the president of the executive board;
    — the power to authorise contracts between the company and a member of the executive or supervisory board.

What are the duties of a director?

A director must execute his duties in a proper and satisfactory way on behalf of the company. General principles have been developed by jurisprudence and doctrine. All members of management, members of the board of directors and members of the executive board must respect provisions of either the law or the articles of association which govern their activities as directors.

Members of the management of a company have special fiduciary duties obliging them to act in the interest of the company. In this context, the PDG may be subject to a restrictive covenant clause. The directors must ensure the proper running of the company.

What are the penalties for a breach of duty by a director?

Directors of either board may incur personal civil and criminal liability in respect of their actions.

Civil liability means that the directors may be sued for damages by someone who has suffered loss through any act or omission on their part.

What is the extent of a director's civil liability?

The civil liability of the board of directors is contained in the following.

- Sections L244 and 249 of the 1966 Act which imposes liability in three main areas:

    — the failure of the directors to respect statutes, for instance provisions governing company procedures such as the calling of shareholder meetings, the preparation of annual accounts or modifying the articles of association;

— the failure to respect articles of association, and in particular the restrictions it places on the directors, on the transfer of shares and on the use of the company's assets;

— the failure to manage the company correctly through negligence, irregular accounts and failure to deal properly with the employees.

● There is also a general liability in the law of torts as set out in ss 1382 and 1383, Code Civil (the French Civil Code).

A director's liability only arises if the company itself or its shareholders or a third party has suffered loss or damage because of the director's fault leading to the loss or damage.

If shareholders or a third party have suffered, then they, as individuals, can make a claim against the directors collectively if it is a collective fault of all the directors, or against individual directors if it is an individual fault.

If the company has suffered, then either a legal representative of the company or a shareholder who holds a certain percentage is entitled to claim.

What is the extent of a director's criminal liability?

The general criminal liability of directors is set out in section 437 of the 1966 Act, which states that certain acts, such as the unauthorised distribution of dividends, the publication of false accounts and acts considered to be contrary to the interests of the company are punishable by fine or imprisonment. Further, there are special provisions governing the criminal liability of directors. For instance, the provisions concerning insider dealing provide for responsibility of directors of a company. Furthermore, employment law contains a special provision known as 'délit d'entrave' which constitutes a liability as to violation of provisions dealing with employees' representation in the company.

What is the liability of a PDG?

A PDG is subject to all the liabilities of a director, as discussed above, together with the added liability which comes with the extra duties of a PDG. Any breach of these duties resulting in loss or damage can result in the PDG being sued.

What about liability of a DG?

A DG is liable for any of his or her personal actions. This criminal liability is equivalent to that of a member of the board of directors.

Is a company liable for a default by its director?

The company itself is primarily liable in civil law for the acts and omissions of its legal representatives (eg directors) under the general principles of tort as set out in s 1382 of the French Civil Code.

However, the company as a legal entity does not have criminal liability. Instead, the legal representatives of the company are subject to criminal liability for any acts or omissions of the company, even if they were not made by the directors themselves. Thus, breach of any of the regulations concerning the company's affairs resulting in insufficient control and imprudent management attracts criminal liability for representatives of the company at director level who may be fined or imprisoned.

Provisions governing penal liability apply to each person, whether or not a director who participated in the management and the representation of the company.

A legal representative of a company is excluded from criminal liability if:

- he or she could not have influenced the act or the person who committed the act;
- the act was committed by a person to whom the whole task had been delegated.

However, the PDG may incur liability, if the PDG him or herself was negligent in choosing the right person or in controlling such person while executing those duties depending on the surrounding circumstances. Further, if the PDG was fully aware of that person's actions he or she might be responsible for any omission to impede the damage.

What is the scope of product liability in France and who is responsible for it?

Product liability is the term used to describe liability imposed on a manufacturer, distributor or seller of a defective product for the damage caused by the defective product either to a person or to someone's property.

A manufacturer, distributor or seller of such a defective product can be held to be civilly liable to the injured party on either a tortious or contractual basis.

First, under the French principle of tort, an injured party can recover damages if he or she can prove that:

- the supplier intentionally or negligently committed an act or omission

relating to the product;
- the injured party suffered a legally recognisable injury; and
- a causal relation exists between the act or omission of the supplier and the damage suffered by the injured party.

Secondly, according to the general principles of French contract law, an injured party may recover damages if he or she can prove that:

- the supplier breached a contractual warranty or obligation;
- the injured party suffered a legally recognisable injury; and
- a causal relation between the breach and the damage exists.

In these cases, the injured party may recover damages from the supplier, ie the company. The company in turn may under special circumstances recover the amount paid to the injured party from the company directors.

Criminal liability only exists where a defective product has caused damage. Usually, because a corporate entity cannot *per se* have any intention to commit an act, a company is not liable to penalties under the criminal law. However, an exception to this general rule exists in the area of product liability and may result in the forced closure of the business or fines for the directors. It should be noted that the Council Directive 85/374 on the harmonisation of the laws concerning liability for a defective product has not yet been implemented in French law. However, the EC Commission has exhorted France to fulfil its obligations under the Treaty.

What are the consequences of company insolvency for a director?

When winding-up proceedings are brought against a company the directors of the company continue to manage the company unless the court directs otherwise. In this instance 'directors' means those people deemed to be managing the company in fact or in law.

A director who carries on operating a company which is insolvent may be liable in several ways.

- The directors may be required to make up part or all of the deficit if managerial errors led to the deficit, provided that the fault of the director is proved. The directors are then jointly and severally liable. Any directors who are liable to contribute to the deficit can be declared bankrupt.
- The court can also declare directors personally bankrupt and they are then prohibited from taking any position as a company director, or engaging either directly or indirectly in any enterprise or business. The duration of the prohibition is fixed by the court and must last for at

least five years. However, such personal bankruptcy will rarely happen unless the director has previously been held liable to contribute to a company's deficit.

What about management and insider dealing in France?

There are two statutes governing insider dealing in France.

- The 'Ordonnance' of 28 September 1967 modified by Law No 89–031 of 2 August 1989 – this provides for criminal sanctions for insider dealing.
- The 'Réglement' No 90–08 of the 'Commission des Opérations de Bourse' (COB) – the COB is a public organisation responsible for the protection of funds invested in securities, listed financial products, negotiable futures and other types of investment which are publicly offered.

Penal sanctions

Whenever an 'insider' deals, or intentionally enables a third party to deal, directly or through a third party in securities listed on a French Stock Exchange on the basis of information which has not been disclosed to the public, he or she is deemed to engage in insider dealing ('délit d'initié') and is subject to penal sanctions (Article 10–1, a11 of the Ordonnance).

The following persons are presumptively deemed to be insiders for the purposes of the foregoing rule: the chairperson of the board of directors; the managing director; the members of the directorate; and the members of the supervisory board. The presumption also applies to their spouses. Other persons are also deemed insiders if, in the course of their activities, they have access to inside information; the burden of proof, however, is placed on the administration. It should be noted that where a legal entity is found to have engaged in insider dealing, its management is held criminally liable for such acts.

The use of insider information is sanctioned by a fine of 6000 to 10 million FFr and/or imprisonment for between two months and two years. In any event, the amount of the fine imposed may not be less than the profits realised from the insider trading and it may be increased beyond the 10 million FFr limit, provided the fine imposed does not exceed ten times the amount of such profits.

In addition, any person who through his professional activities or duties possesses inside information and conveys such information to a third party outside the context of such activities or duties is liable to a fine of 10,000–100,000 FFr and/or imprisonment from one to six months.

Administrative Sanctions
Under the 'Réglement', the COB introduced several restrictions in relation
to insider dealing. These apply to members of the issuing organisations as
well as all other persons who receive insider information as a result of their
involvement in the preparation or performance of financial operations or
who receive such information for professional reasons. Anyone who comes
within any of these categories is prohibited not only from using but also
from disclosing such information. If they do disclose information, the
person to whom the information is disclosed is prohibited from using that
information, although he or she will not be liable merely for disclosing it
to a third party. Any person breaching any of these provisions may be
subject to a fine of up to 10 million FFr.

How does an individual cease to be a director?
A director can be removed from his or her position for the following
reasons.

- When his term of office as a director ends. Usually the term of office is
  fixed in the articles. However, this term may not exceed in the case of a
  member of the board of directors:

  — three years, if directors are appointed by the articles;
  — six years, if the directors are appointed by the shareholders' meeting.
  In the case of a member of the executive board, the duration of the term
  of office may be fixed by the articles at a period of between two and six
  years – if this is not done then his term will end after four years.

- When the company itself ceases to operate.
- If the director is removed from this position (eg by the shareholders).
- If the director resigns.

How may a member of the board of directors of an SA resign or be dismissed?
Directors of an SA may be dismissed at any moment and without any
reason. However, if the director can establish that his or her removal was
made in an injurious and vexatious manner, he or she may claim damages.

A director can resign without any real reason, but may then be liable to
a possible claim for damages by the company if he or she resigned in order
to damage the company. A director is obliged to resign if he or she loses
full mental capacity or if he or she is the director of more than eight
companies or exceeds the age limit.

How may a PDG be dismissed?

A PDG may be dismissed at any stage by the board. In the event that the PDG is removed without cause, he or she may bring a suit against the corporation but only where his or her removal was made in an injurious and vexatious manner.

How is a DG dismissed?

The DG may be removed by the board on the recommendation of the PDG.

What about the removal of members of the executive board?

A member of the executive board can only be removed if there is a substantive reason and the removal is carried out by the shareholders in general meeting on the proposal of the supervisory board. If there is no justification for the removal, the member of the executive board can claim damages.

Removal from the executive board does not necessarily invalidate the contract of employment and this will also have to be dealt with.

The supervisory board can itself remove a president from this position but not from his or her role as a director.

Members of the executive board may resign at any time.

MANAGEMENT OF A Sàrl

Are the requirements for the management structure of a Sàrl the same as in the case of an SA?

No. A Sàrl is managed by a number of 'Gérants', (usually one or two), who are referred to throughout as business-managers. They run the business and are broadly equivalent to a PDG of an SA.

It would theoretically be possible for a Sàrl to be controlled by a supervisory board, but in practice this rarely happens.

Who can be a business-manager of a Sàrl?

The business-manager of a Sàrl need not be a shareholder, unless the articles of association so provide.

Who is excluded from being a business-manager of a Sàrl?

The following persons are not allowed to become a business-manager of a Sàrl:

- corporate persons;

- legally incapacitated persons;
- the auditors of the company (and this prohibition lasts for five years after the auditor steps down from this position);
- any person who exceeds the age limit provided by the articles of association. There are no rules concerning the age limit of business-managers but one could argue that the age limit for a director of an SA, eg 65 years, could apply analogously;
- any person who is guilty of a crime which has, as one of its penalties, the prohibition from being a business manager of a Sàrl.

It should be noted that on 31 December 1990 a new law was passed as to the exercise of an independent profession in the form of a company. It is now possible for members of independent professions such as lawyers, surgeons or architects to establish a 'Société d'exercice liberal à responsabilité limitée' (SELARL) which is a form of Sàrl, a 'Sociéte d'exercice liberal à forme anonyme' (SELAFA) corresponding to an SA or a 'Société d'exercice liberal en commandite par actions' (SELCA). The managers of such companies must be members of the profession which is the object of the company. This new law will be in force as from 1 January 1992.

As in the case of an SA, the articles of association may provide that only French and EC nationals may be business-managers of a Sàrl. Further, business-managers who are not nationals of an EC member state must request a professional card ('carte de commerçant').

Who appoints the business-manager of a Sàrl?

The business-manager of a Sàrl can be appointed as follows:

- when the company is formed, the business-manager is appointed by the articles of association or by a special decision of the shareholders;
- at any other time, the business-manager is appointed by the shareholders in general meeting by a majority decision.

When a person is offered the position of a business-manager, he or she must declare his or her acceptance of the office.

May a business-manager have a service agreement with the company?

Yes, but the following conditions apply:

- the business-manager should not be a majority shareholder in the company;
- the service agreement must be a legally binding contract and not simply

a device designed to avoid the particular rules relating to the dismissal of business-managers;

● there must be a difference between the office of a business manager and the technical role, ie his or her special job for which he or she must receive distinct remuneration.

When a valid service agreement exists, the business-manager of a Sàrl has a dual role: he or she is an officer of the company who can be removed from this position by the shareholders and he or she is also an employee. The service agreement gives the business-manager the usual legal protection of an employee such as a minimum holiday allowance, the right to damages for dismissal and national insurance.

How is the business-manager rewarded?

The remuneration of the business-manager of a Sàrl is fixed by the articles of association or by shareholders' resolution. If no remuneration has been fixed, it can be determined by a court. Again, as in the case of a PDG of the SA, the remuneration may be linked to the turnover and/or profit of the company. The business-manager will also be able to claim back any reasonable expenses.

Are there any restrictions on benefits which a business-manager can receive from the company?

As is the case for the director of an SA, the business-manager of a Sàrl must not receive any loan, any overdraft protection or any other form of security from the company (s 51 of the 1966 Act.)

Further, any other contracts concluded between the company and the business-manager conferring any advantage on the latter are subject to approval by the shareholders unless the negotiation concerns a matter which is customary for the parties alone to decide.

What tax contributions must be paid by a business-manager?

The taxation of the business-manager's remuneration depends on whether or not he or she is a minority or a majority shareholder in the company.

The salary of a majority business-manager is taxed in the industrial and commercial income category.

The salary of a minority business-manager is taxed in the wages and salaries category. In this category a deduction of 10 per cent is made for professional fees. In addition, there exists a further special deduction of 20 per cent which decreases to 10 per cent if the business-manager holds directly or indirectly 35 per cent of the company's share capital, and if his or her salary exceeds an amount which is fixed by decree. If the salary exceeds 588,000FFr per year, there is no special deduction at all.

Must a business-manager contribute to a social security plan?
This depends on whether he or she is a majority or minority business-manager.

- A majority business-manager is not obliged to affiliate to the general employees' social security mechanism. However, he or she is obliged to affiliate to the special social security category for members of independent professions or employers.
- A minority business-manager or a business-manager holding a certain percentage of shares is obliged to contribute to the general social security system if he or she receives a remuneration. If he or she does not receive any remuneration he or she is not obliged to affiliate to either the general employee nor to the special employee social security system.

What is the basis of a business manager's authority?
Like a director of an SA, the business-manager derives his or her authority from the following sources:

- from statute, ie the 1966 Act and the 1967 Decree;
- the articles of association;
- shareholders' decisions, and any other special rules.

What are the powers of a business-manager?
According to s 49, sub-s 4 of the 1966 Act, the business-manager is the legal representative of the Sàrl. He or she therefore has wide powers to represent, negotiate for and commit the company to third parties. The powers of a Sàrl business-manager are derived from shareholder decisions and these are themselves restricted by the articles of association.

If the articles of association do not restrict the powers of the business-manager, then he or she has the power to act for the company on all matters within its objects according to s 49, sub-section 5 of the 1966 Act.

If a company has several business-managers, they may act separately, and have separate responsibilities and consequent liability, unless the articles of association provide otherwise.

How are the powers of a business-manager restricted?
The powers of a business-manager of a Sàrl can be restricted:

- by the articles of association which may provide that prior authorisation of the shareholders in general meeting is needed before certain contracts can be entered into or certain large transactions which are of importance to the company can be completed;
- the business-manager must act within the objects of the company;
- if the Sàrl has a supervisory board the business manager must respect its authority;
- a similar restriction exists between a Sàrl business-manager and the company as exists between the director of an SA and the company in respect of contracts made between the director and the company (see above).

What are the duties of a business-manager?

Like directors of an SA, the business-manager must respect the statutes and contractual agreements which determine his or her relationship with the company and third persons, and has the same fiduciary duties to act in the company's interest. Like the PDG, the business-manager may be subject to a restrictive covenant clause.

What are the penalties for a breach of duty by the business-manager?

Like the director of an SA, the business-manager may be subject to civil and/or criminal liability.

Civil liability may arise if he or she acts in contravention of legal provisions of the articles, or if he or she generally mismanages the company. A claim can be brought either by an individual or by the company.

Criminal liability is described in ss 4 and 5 of the 1966 Act and is similar to the criminal responsibility of the directors of an SA.

Is a Sàrl liable for the default of its business-manager?

The rules applicable to an SA are also valid for a Sàrl. Therefore, the company is liable according to the general principles of tort for acts of its legal representatives.

Do the same rules as in the case of an SA apply to a business-manager of a Sàrl for product liability?

Yes. The general rules governing civil and criminal liability for defective products are applicable to a business-manager.

What about insolvency of the company?

The business-manager of a Sàrl is subject to the same provisions as a director of an SA (see above).

How may a business-manager of a Sàrl be dismissed?

According to s 55 of the 1966 Act a business-manager can be removed by a simple majority in a shareholders' resolution. If this removal is without a substantive justifiable reason, then the business-manager may claim damages.

Furthermore, a business-manager may be removed by the court at the instigation of any shareholder if the court feels that there is sufficient reason to do so.

How may the business-manager resign?

The resignation of a business-manager must be notified to all shareholders of the company.

GERMANY

Hans Schimmelpfennig

What are the main types of company which exist in Germany?
The two main forms of company in Germany which must appoint directors are:

- the stock corporation or 'Aktiengesellschaft', referred to as 'AG';
- the limited liability company 'Gesellschaft mit beschränkter Haftung', – referred to as 'GmbH'.

Is the stock corporation (AG) a public company?
Yes, the stock corporation is a public company governed by the Stock Corporation Act (Aktiengesetz). This is the most suitable structure for large businesses needing a sizeable capital base and may be established by five or more persons. Its minimum share capital must be at least 100,000DM and is divided into shares of at least 50DM each. The AG may be quoted on the Stock Exchange.

Although when an AG is formed it must comply with the regulations and provisions of the Stock Corporation Act, the provisions of the Stock Exchange Act (Börsengesetz) only apply if the AG is to go public in Germany.

Are there any variations of an AG?
Yes, although rarely used in practice, there is the KGaA(Kommaditgesellschaft; Gesetz Aktien). This combines the characteristics of the stock corporation and a limited partnership, and involves unlimited liability for at least one of the participants.

What about the structure of the private limited liability company?
The GmbH is a private company governed by the GmbH Act. The GmbH is mostly used by smaller businesses as it is both cheaper and less complex to administer than the stock corporation. Such a company must have a minimum of one shareholder. Its share capital must be at least 50,000DM and is divided into shares of at least 500DM each. Each shareholder may only hold one share of the capital at the time of the establishment of the company. He may, however, acquire other shares from other shareholders during the company's life. A GmbH is frequently appointed as general

partner in a limited partnership ('GmbH & Co KG') which makes it possible to restrict the unlimited personal liability of the general partner to the registered capital of a (limited) company, ie the GmbH.

MANAGEMENT OF AN AG

What are the requirements for the management structure of an AG?
An AG must have two different boards of directors; an executive board and a supervisory board.

- The executive board is known as the 'Vorstand'. It is responsible for the management and the day-to-day business of the company and therefore deals with third parties on behalf of the company.
- The supervisory or controlling board is the 'Aufsichtsrat'. Its main function is to appoint and to remove the members of the executive board, and to observe and control the way in which the executive board manages the business of the company. The supervisory board represents the company in judicial and extrajudicial matters against the members of the executive board. The supervisory function is granted to the supervisory board as such and not to its individual members. A lawsuit may therefore only be initiated by the board collectively and not by special members, eg the employees' representatives.

The management structure of an AG is explained below.

How many directors must an AG have?
An AG must have at least one director. If such a company has an authorised share capital of more than 3 million DM, the company must have two directors unless the articles of association provide otherwise. The board may have a chairperson appointed by the supervisory board, but if no chairperson is appointed, the executive board may appoint a representative or speaker ('Sprecher'). Banks especially favour the appointment of a speaker. The company may also have junior directors (ie deputy members of the executive board). There is no difference between a deputy member and an ordinary member of the executive board. They basically have equal status as regards their legal powers of representation and management.

Are there any special requirements for appointments to the executive board?
Yes. In AGs, which are subject to the Co-determination Acts 1951 or 1976, a labour director or 'Arbeitsdirektor' who is in charge of personal and social matters must also be appointed.

When are the Co-determination Acts applicable?

There are three Acts to consider. Usually these are collectively referred as 'the Co-determination Acts':

- the Co-determination Act 1976 ('Mitbestimmungsgesetz'), which is applicable in the case of an AG, a KGaA, a GmbH or a mining company with more than 2000 employees.
- the Co-determination Act 1951 ('Montanmitbestimmungsgesetz'), which is applicable if the AG or GmbH is an enterprise in the mining, steel or iron business and if it has more than 1000 employees;
- the Shop Constitution Act 1952 ('Betriebsverfassungsgesetz'), which is applicable to any AG or KGaA (except a family concern with less than 500 employees) and any GmbH with more than 500 employees.

What about supervisory boards of AGs?

The supervisory board of an AG must have at least 3 members. The articles of association may provide for a higher number which must be divisible by three and must not exceed the maximum number of 21 members permitted under the Stock Corporation Act. (The maximum number varies depending upon the level of the share capital – see below.)

Is the structure of the supervisory board always the same?

No, the structure of the supervisory board can be affected by the Co-determination Acts, where these are applicable. If the Acts are applicable, the supervisory board consists of representatives of both shareholders and employees, otherwise it only consists of shareholders.

Who can be a director?

Any individual person who is not legally incapacitated may be a director of an AG. A foreign national may act as a director of the executive board, as well as of the supervisory board.

Who is excluded from being a director?

The following persons are prohibited from being directors on the executive board:

- members of the supervisory board;
- persons who are disqualified by a court order or the decision of a public authority from the exercise of a certain occupation or trade, as far as the prohibition corresponds to the object of the enterprise;
- persons who have been adjudged bankrupt or who have been guilty of

certain criminal acts relating to insolvency within the previous five years from the date of the judgment;
- companies and other legal entities.

Who appoints directors in an AG?

The members of the executive board are appointed by the supervisory board with a five-year term. Thereafter reappointment is possible, but must be effected by a specific decision of the supervisory board.

Is there a register of directors?

No, but there is a local register of companies at a designated local court and the details of directors can be found on this.

How do you find out which court is designated for the registration of a large company?

According to the Stock Corporation Act, and unless otherwise provided for in the articles of association, it is the court at the place where the central place of business or the head office of the company is situated.

What is the relationship between the company and the director in an AG?

A member of the executive board has two kinds of relationship with the company, as follows.

- As an 'organ' of the company, he is empowered to conduct its business and to represent the company independent of the supervisory board and of the shareholders. Requests made by the shareholders in general meeting or the supervisory board are only one aspect of the decision-making process. The only criterion to guide the executive board members is that they must act in the best interests of the company, ie the executive board is independent of both the shareholders and third parties.
- Various rights and duties arise between the director and the company, and these are usually defined in a service agreement. This is a contract under civil law. Under ss 611 and 675 of the Civil Code, the director is obliged to render services for the company and the company to pay remuneration. If there is no service agreement, the relationship is determined in accordance with the general principles of the 'mandate' (s 662), under which no remuneration is payable to the director but the director none the less owes duties to the company.

Who are the parties to a director's service contract?

The service agreement is concluded between the director and the supervisory board. It usually includes the director's obligation to direct the company and further provisions concerning his working hours, job description, power of attorney, competition and confidentiality clauses, social clauses such as retirement and surviving dependant's benefits, and remuneration and holiday entitlements.

The term of a service agreement may not exceed five years. This period corresponds to the term of appointment of the director by the supervisory board (s 84 of the Stock Corporation Act), as otherwise the decision of the supervisory board to appoint the members of the board of directors could be influenced. The contract may contain a clause providing that the contract can be renewed after five years. It can also be agreed upon from the beginning that, in the case of a new appointment, the service agreement shall automatically be extended on expiration of the first term.

How is the director of an AG rewarded?

The remuneration of a director may consist of a salary, profit-sharing arrangements, repayment of expenses incurred by him in relation to the company's affairs and life assurance, as well as commissions and other performance-related payments.

According to s 87 of the Stock Corporation Act, the remuneration of the director of an AG must be in reasonable proportion to the responsibilities of the director concerned and the current financial health of the company. The remuneration is fixed by the supervisory board.

The Act also prescribes the basis for the calculation of any profit-sharing arrangements (which may be modified by the articles of association) but, in general terms, this is the profit after deduction of the losses carried forward from the preceding financial year and the reserves formed out of profits.

Are there any restrictions on the benefits which a director can receive from a company?

Loans to directors of an AG may only be made with the approval of the supervisory board. A supervisory board resolution is required for a specific loan facility or similar transaction and may not be given in advance for a period exceeding three months. The interest and the conditions for reimbursement of the loan must be fixed. If the loan is paid to a director without the approval of the supervisory board, it must be repaid immediately, unless the supervisory board gives subsequent approval, in which case the grant of the loan will retrospectively be deemed to have been approved by the supervisory board from the outset. If the company is a bank, additional and complex rules are imposed by the provisions of the Banking Act or 'Gesetz über das Kreditwesen'.

Is a director of an AG an employee of the company?

The director of an AG is not regarded as an employee of the company as there is no so-called 'social dependence'. A director is the head of the company and, unlike an employee, is not subject to control and directions.

What tax and social security contributions must be paid by a director of an AG?

Tax contributions

Remuneration paid to directors is taxed as income tax.

A non-resident director, eg a director who is not domiciled in Germany or whose presence in Germany does not exceed six months per annum, is taxed on his German source income (domestic income) in Germany. If the director is resident in Germany, he may be taxed on his worldwide income, although this may be subject to the provisions of double taxation treaties.

Social security

The members of the board of an AG are not generally subject to social security contributions because they are not in socially dependent employment. If members do not benefit from the social security system, some social protection is derived from the 'special relationship of mutual responsibility and loyalty' between director and company, – eg sufficient time for holidays, or continued payment of remuneration in case of illness. Further social insurance benefits are frequently provided for by the service agreement, eg retirement benefits, provisions for surviving dependants, accident insurance and support in the case of sickness.

From where does a company director of an AG derive his authority?

The powers of directors are derived from:

- statutory regulations, ie principally the Stock Corporation Act;
- the articles of association, which may determine the powers of the board, but which may not overrule or replace the special division of powers between the different organs of the company;
- other agreements, special rules and shareholder decisions.

What are the main powers of a director of an AG?

The board of directors has two main powers which are derived from ss 76–8 of the Stock Corporation Act.

- Directors are collectively responsible for the direction of the affairs and business of the company independently of direct shareholder control.
- They represent the company in dealings with third parties. This power includes the right to sign on behalf of the company and thereby contractually bind it, and cannot be restricted in relation to dealings with third parties.

Does the board have to act by consent?

Yes. If the board consists of several members, they have to act by unanimous consent, unless the articles of association enable a majority decision.

Although the law provides that the company must be represented by all appointed directors collectively, the articles of association may provide that a lesser number may represent the company. This has to be entered in the commercial register.

In addition, the Act requires:

- the preparation and the execution of resolutions decided on at the general meeting of the shareholders (s 83 of the Stock Corporation Act);
- a yearly or, in some cases, quarterly report to the supervisory board about the board's activities, the economic situation and the course of the company's affairs (s 90 of the Stock Corporation Act);
- the production of the annual accounts and financial reports of the company.

How are the powers of a director restricted?

Specific restrictions on the power of directors *vis à vis* the company may be:

- statutory; or
- contractual; or
- imposed by the control of the supervisory board.

What are the statutory restrictions on the powers of directors of an AG?

The Stock Corporation Act contains a number of restrictions. These can be divided into two groups.

The first group of restrictions relates to matters which require the board of directors to act in concert with the supervisory board. It concerns the representation of the company in court in actions to challenge the validity of resolutions of the shareholders in general meeting or to declare the company a nullity.

The second group of restrictions relates to transactions requiring the approval of the shareholders in general meeting. For example, the settlement or termination of:

- damages claims brought by the company against the Board of Directors or Supervisory Board in relation to the setting up of the company; or
- general claims against members of the executive or supervisory boards

  — making claims against shareholders or others who have improperly used their influence on the directors to the detriment of the company,
  — resolutions for the issue of convertible debentures,
  — the conclusion and modification of a contract creating special relationships with other companies, eg intercompany agreements,
  — mergers with other companies,
  — all transfers of assets as a whole which do not constitute a merger or which are not otherwise separately regulated by statute are subject to s 361 Stock Corporation Act and therefore require the consent of the shareholders in general meeting,
  — the transfer of a substantial part of the company's assets to a public corporation,
  — transfers in any other form and the transformation of a private into a public company.

Are there any other restrictions?

Yes, the Stock Corporation Act (s 88) provides that any activity of a director in the same area of business as the company, the appointment of a director as a director of another company or his appointment as an unlimited partner in a partnership, requires the approval of the supervisory board.

There is a further restriction contained in s 32 of Mitbestimmung Gesetz (Mit Best G) 1176 which requires a member of the executive board to obtain the consent of the supervisory board to participate in a company subject to the Co-determination Act.

What about insider dealing?

The members of both boards are subject to the provisions of the Criminal law governing insider dealing, and also guidelines on insider trading issued by the Minister of Economics following recommendations from a panel of Stock Exchange experts and the Ministry of Finance. These guidelines give rise to civil liability and, unlike the general Criminal law, are only binding to the extent to which parties agree. The guidelines prohibit persons dealing in securities where they may have insider information.

Under EC law, the new directive relating to insider dealing obliges the Member States to adopt its provisions by 1 June 1992 at the latest. Germany will then have statutory regulations governing insider dealing.

What are the most usual contractual restrictions on the director of an AG?

The company's constitution embodies the rights and duties of its participants, and takes effect in German law as a contract. This means that articles of association ('the Articles') must be construed according to the general principles of contract law.

The articles may restrict the power to carry on the business, but not the power to represent the company to third persons. They may also provide that certain decisions are subject to supervisory board approval. However, transactions of the board of directors are not subject to the approval of the shareholders in general meeting, unless this is specifically requested by the directors.

What further control exists over directors?

As stated above, the management of a company by the directors can be controlled by the supervisory board. This is obligatory in all AGs.

Does the number of members of a supervisory board vary?

Yes. According to the Stock Corporation Act, s 95:

- A company having an authorised share capital of up to 3 million DM may have up to 9 members;
- if the share capital exceeds 3 million DM, the company may have up to 15 members;
- in the case of a company with a share capital of more than 20 million DM there may be up to 21 members.

The maximum number of members must not be exceeded.

When must the supervisory board include employee representatives?

If the Shop Constitution Act 1952 is applicable (see above), one-third of the members of the supervisory board must be employees' representatives.

The supervisory board of a company under the Co-determination Act 1951 (steel and mining industry) must have 11 members, of which 5 must be members of the shareholders and 5 must be members of the employees, as well as 1 neutral member.

Under the Co-determination Act 1976, companies with up to 10,000 employees must have a supervisory board with 12 members; from 10,000 up to 20,000 employees, 16 members; and in the case of more than 20,000 employees, 20 members. The members are divided equally into representatives of the employees and/or representatives of the shareholders. Due to the method of electing a chairperson and the chairman's right to the casting vote in the case of an equality of the votes, the shareholders' predominant influence in the supervisory board is secured.

Who can be a member of a supervisory board?

In contrast to the regulations concerning the membership of the executive board, all individuals (including adjudicated bankrupts) can be members of the supervisory board, with the exception of:

- members of the board of directors;
- legal representatives of a dependent company;
- legal representatives of a second company in which one member of the executive board of directors is a member of the supervisory board;
- individuals who are members of more than nine other supervisory boards.

Who appoints the members of a supervisory board?

The members coming from the shareholders' side are elected by the shareholders themselves. The employees' representatives are elected in accordance with the requirements of the applicable Co-determination Act. The articles of association can provide rights for certain shareholders holding a specified number of shares to appoint a member of the supervisory board. The members can be removed at any stage by a three-quarters majority decision. Moreover, a member of the supervisory board can be removed for important reasons by way of a court decision; the supervisory board decides on the filing of such an application by simple majority.

What is the relationship between a company and the members of the supervisory board?

The relationship between members of the supervisory board and the company is determined by statute and/or the articles of association, and additional agreements covering specific points of concern. Payment of the members of the supervisory board is in accordance with the articles of association or by resolution in a shareholders' meeting.

What are their duties?
All supervisory board members, whether representatives of the shareholders or the employees, owe the duty of care and diligence of a conscientious manager to the company. They also have a fiduciary duty and an obligation to maintain secrecy. This duty and the sanctions for a breach of duty are similar to those applicable to an executive board director, as the main provisions for directors contained in s 93 of the Stock Corporation Act are by analogy applicable to a member of a supervisory board (see below).

What are their powers?
Members of the supervisory board have the following powers:

- appointment and revocation of the members of the executive board of directors;
- control over the activity of the board of directors and therefore examination of records and accounts generally;
- representation of the company's interests in matters concerning members of the executive board;
- calling of a shareholders' meeting if this is required in the interest of the company;
- examination of the annual accounts and reporting thereon at the shareholders' meeting.

What are the duties of a director?
Special duties regarding the manner of execution of a director's duties, as distinct from the duties themselves, are imposed by the Stock Corporation Act. Thus, under s 93, the director of an AG must act with the proper and conscientious diligence of a manager of a company. This includes a duty of loyalty to the company and a duty of non-competition.

If, according to the balance sheet, there is a loss of half of the share capital, the board has to call the shareholders' meeting without delay in order to report on such loss. In the case of insolvency or indebtedness, the board has to file a bankruptcy petition (or a petition with the court for institution of composition proceedings) not later than three weeks from the occurrence of the event. A violation of these duties constitutes a criminal offence.

In addition, if the director has a special service agreement with the company, he must respect the general and specific contractual duties in the agreement, in particular the duty of care and competence.

What liability does an executive board director of an AG face for a breach of duty?

Directors may be subject to both civil and criminal liability.

Civil liability

This concerns the directors' liability for damage caused by their fault arising out of the mismanagement of the company or improper executive action. Civil action may be taken against a director by the company itself (through the supervisory board), a company's creditor, its shareholders or the tax authorities.

Criminal liability

This is enforced by a prosecution brought by the public authorities responsible for criminal acts against the individual member or members of the executive board. A successful prosecution can result in a fine or imprisonment. However, certain economic and tax provisions allow for the imposition of a fine on a stock corporation itself.

By what standard is a director judged?

Any breach by a director of his duty of diligence makes him liable for any damage incurred by the company, unless he can prove that he has acted with the diligence of a proper and conscientious member of the board, such diligence being judged in accordance with an objective test. However, it is possible for the company to relieve a director of liability under s 93, although this can only occur after the expiration of three years from the date the claim arose and is subject to the consent of a majority of more than 90 per cent of the shareholders in general meeting. The director shall not be liable pursuant to s 93 of the Stock Corporation Act if the action is based on a prior lawful decision of the shareholders' meeting.

What is a director's liability under the Stock Corporation Act?

A director may, notwithstanding anything contained in the articles, have a residual liability under s 93 to creditors of the company if the company has not satisfied its claim in full. However, in practice this general provision is rarely used.

What about anti-competitive behaviour?

The directors of an AG may be liable for any breach of the obligations resulting from s 88 of the Stock Corporation Act, concerning the duty of non-competition.

Is a director liable for tortious acts of his company?

The director of an AG may also be made liable under the general rules for torts, such as s 823 II of the Civil Code, together with the protective legislative provisions. The company, the shareholders and third persons are all granted rights of action against a director, as opposed to the company itself, under these provisions.

What about tax?

Directors are liable to tax authorities under ss 34 and 69 Abgabenordnung (AO) (general tax code). As the legal representatives of a company, they are responsible for the declaration of the company's revenues and the payment of tax, and they may be personally liable for a wilful or grossly negligent breach of these duties.

How can a director incur criminal liability?

Under criminal law, the directors are liable for:

- general fraudulent and dishonest acts under s 266 of the Penal Code;
- deception under s 263 of the Penal Code;
- specific criminal liability, including breaches of the provisions relating to declarations in respect of the share capital and the economic situation of the company, or breaches of duties relating to insolvent liquidation of the company prescribed by the Stock Corporation Act (ss 399–404);
- other offences applicable to members of the executive and supervisory boards are specified in s 405 of the Stock Corporation Act.

Is a company liable for the default of its directors?

A company itself may be liable to third parties for damages resulting from acts of the directors committed in the course of their duties. This is a general rule for corporations, contained in s 31 of the German Civil Code.

What is product liability and who is liable for it?

Under German law product liability arises in the following situations.

- In negligence, whereby the supplier of products is liable for any damage to health, body, life or property of an ultimate buyer or the buyer in tort, s 823 of the German Civil Code.
- Since 1 January 1990 there is additional liability under the 'Produkt-haftungsgesetz', implementing the EC product liability directive, which introduced strict liability for damage caused to a consumer. Under its provisions third parties, who must be consumers, have a right of action arising out of injuries caused and, in addition, the ultimate buyer (also a

consumer) of the defective goods has a right to recover for damage to his property.

Can a director be liable for product liability?

Except where such liability arises out of the direct fault of a director, the company is liable (s 31 of the German Civil Code).

What are the consequences of company insolvency for a director of an AG?

In the case of a company insolvency, the following reporting duties must be respected.

● In the case of a loss or cessation of payments, the board of directors must call an extraordinary meeting of the shareholders if there is a loss of capital of an amount equal to half the authorised share capital of the company (s 92 of the Stock Corporation Act).
● If the company is insolvent the directors must immediately, and in any event within three months after the insolvency, declare the company's bankruptcy or propose a settlement (s 92(2) of the Stock Corporation Act).
● An insolvency petition may be filed by the directors, the creditors or the liquidator (s 208 of the Insolvency Act).

The filing of the petition results in the dissolution of the company. Insolvency is essentially the inability of a company to pay its debts.

What is a director's position in the case of insolvency?

As soon as bankruptcy proceedings have begun, the company is considered to be in liquidation. Contrary to the liquidation procedure as provided for by the Stock Corporation Act (in which a corporate director may act as liquidator), under the Insolvency Act, an administrator ('Konkursverwalter') is appointed by the court to act as liquidator. The result of this is that the directors no longer carry out the day-to-day running of the company which must thereafter be undertaken by the administrator.

The Insolvency Act procedure does not automatically terminate the director's office or service agreement. This is in contrast to bankruptcy proceedings, where the members of the executive board always lose their power of representation. However, where the company is insolvent, the administrator has the power to terminate the director's service agreement and any such termination automatically constitutes good cause which justifies the removal of an executive board member by the supervisory board. On the other hand, in the case of a company which has gone bankrupt, any member of the executive board may both resign from office and terminate his employment with the company.

It should be noted there is no distinction between a creditors' winding-up or a liquidator being appointed.

How can a director of an AG be dismissed?
The supervisory board has the power to dismiss a director.

Dismissal before the end of the term by the supervisory board is only possible for a substantial reason (s 84(3) of the Stock Corporation Act). The Act defines this as including a serious breach of duty, incapacity to manage the company or a vote of no confidence by the shareholders.

How does dismissal affect a director's service agreement?
It is important to realise that the conditions justifying termination of the service agreement are different to those justifying the removal of a director as an officer of the company. As a director's service agreement and the office of director are legally independent the service agreement does not automatically terminate when he ceases to be an officer of the company. There can only be termination for good cause, although any material breach of contract which is serious constitutes good cause justifying termination. As the director is not an employee of the company, the provisions applicable to employees containing special protection against dismissal do not apply, although notice of termination of the service agreement must be given within two weeks of the date on which the supervisory board becomes aware of the breach.

What is the procedure for resignation by a director of an AG?
He may resign his office after having given due notice terminating the service agreement (German Civil Code).

What is the position of a director who has not been properly appointed?
When a person acts as a director, but either has not been properly appointed or has an invalid service contract, there are special rules which govern his position in the company. If he acts as a director with the knowledge of the other directors or the supervisory board, then the duties of an ordinary director will be imposed on him. If he represents the company in relation to third parties with the knowledge of the board, then those third parties will be bound by any contract or agreement entered

into with him, unless they knew at that time that he did not have the full capacity of a director of the company.

What happens if a required member of the executive board is missing or the supervisory board does not have the necessary number of members?

In urgent cases, the court may appoint a member of the executive board until the missing member is appointed in another manner. The court may also complete the necessary number of the members of the supervisory board upon request of the executive board, a member of the supervisory board or a shareholder.

MANAGEMENT OF A GMBH

Who is responsible for managing a GmbH?

The day-to-day business of a GmbH is run not by directors as such, but by one or more 'managing directors' ('Geschäftsführer'), who are controlled by the shareholders. There are no restrictions on the minimum or maximum numbers of managing directors that a company may have, although a company or corporation cannot itself be a managing director. The company may also have junior directors who follow the same rules as the ordinary directors.

Are the requirements for the management structure of a GmbH the same as for an AG?

No. In principle, there is no requirement for a GmbH to have a supervisory board, although the articles of association may provide for a supervisory board. The Articles may also provide for other structures such as an advisory board or a shareholders' committee. As there are no legal regulations applicable to these bodies, their functions have to be stated in the articles of association.

What about GmbHs with more than 500 employees?

A GmbH with over 500 employees must appoint a supervisory board in accordance with statutes generally known as the Co-determination Acts which aim to protect and formally represent the rights of employees.

Are there any provisions applicable to the members of the supervisory board of a GmbH if a supervisory board is appointed?

If a supervisory board has been appointed in a GmbH, either by the shareholders or in accordance with the Co-determination Acts, its constitution and number of members will be determined by the articles or by the Act, as appropriate. If the articles of the GmbH are deficient, then the provisions of the Stock Corporation Act will apply (see above).

Who can be a managing director?
As is the case with an AG, any natural person, who is not legally incapacitated, may be a managing director of a GmbH, including foreign nationals.

Who is excluded from being a managing director?
The rules for members of an executive board also apply to the managing directors of a GmbH. Therefore, the same persons are excluded as for the board of an AG.

Who appoints the managing directors of a GmbH?
Managing directors of a GmbH are appointed by a resolution of the shareholders in general meeting, except where the Co-determination Acts 1951 and 1976 apply, in which case the supervisory board is empowered to appoint the managing directors.

The articles of association may, however, provide that another body such as an advisory board, shareholders' committee or a certain shareholder is competent to appoint a managing director.

For how long can a GmbH managing director serve?
The GmbH Act does not specify the duration of the managing director's office and he may therefore be appointed without a time limit. If the Co-determination Acts 1951 or 1976 apply, the managing director may be appointed only for five years, according to s 84 of the Stock Corporation Act (see above).

What is the position of a managing director of a GmbH?
In relation to his representing and acting for the company, a managing director is in the same position as a director. He is not in a relationship of social dependence to the company. He is the person who carries on the business of the company and is empowered to deal with all commercial and technical matters.

A managing director may have a service agreement similar to an agreement with a director of an AG (see above).

Who are the parties to a GmbH managing director's service contract?
In the case of a GmbH *without* a supervisory board, the contract is made between the managing director and the shareholders. In the case of a

GmbH *with* a supervisory board, it is concluded between the managing director and the members of the board.

As with the appointment of the managing director, the articles of association may provide that another person or a certain shareholder may conclude the service agreement.

How is a managing director of a GmbH rewarded?
The GmbH Act does not contain any rules governing the remuneration of managing directors. The obligation to pay the managing director can be contained either in a service agreement or in the articles of association, but a managing director may render his services without any remuneration. No special rules exist governing the calculation of profit sharing.

What about loans to managing directors of a GmbH?
Section 43a of the GmbH Act prohibits a company from making loans to its managing directors and certain other persons if capital necessary for the protection of the authorised share capital would be used. Any loan paid to the managing director in breach of s 43a of the GmbH Act must be immediately reimbursed to the company.

What tax and social security contributions must be paid by a managing director of a GmbH?
The tax contributions to be paid by a managing director are the same as for a director of an AG (see above).

A managing director of a GmbH having a service agreement with the company may be subject to the social security system:

- if he renders services to the company; and
- if he receives remuneration for such services; and
- if he does not exercise a dominant influence upon the company, eg as a majority shareholder.

Therefore, if the managing director does not receive remuneration, or if he only carries out his duty resulting from the special corporate relationship with the company, he is not liable for any social security contributions. The same applies to a managing director who is a majority shareholder. For this reason, the managing director in a 'one man GmbH' and directors who hold more than 50 per cent of the share capital are not obliged to contribute to social security. Additional benefits may be afforded in the service agreement, eg insurance, retirement benefits and surviving dependants' benefits.

From where does a managing director of a GmbH derive his authority?

The powers of a managing director are determined by the GmbH Act, and by certain contractual agreements such as the articles of association and the service agreement. His legal authority may not be restricted in relation to dealings with third parties, but may be cut down in internal dealings.

What are the powers of a managing director of a GmbH?

As with the director of an AG, the managing director of a GmbH manages and represents the company in dealings with third parties (s 35 of the GmbH Act). However, in managing the affairs of the company, the managing director is subject to the directions of the shareholders.

What must a managing director do?

The Act provides that the managing directors must do the following, *inter alia*:

- They must prepare the annual accounts of the company for each financial year and present them to the shareholders who approve them in general meeting (s 42a of the GmbH Act). The annual accounts of the company must be submitted to the Registry Court in accordance with the commercial code.
- They must present, together with the accounts, a list signed by the managing directors, containing the surnames, first names, marital status and addresses of all individual shareholders, as well as the number of their shares (s 40 of the GmbH Act).
- They must, in the case of insolvency or indebtedness, file a bankruptcy petition or a petition with the court for institution of composition proceedings without delay, but not later than three weeks from the occurrence of one of these events.
- They must immediately call a shareholders' meeting if it becomes obvious that half the share capital has been lost.

How are the powers of a managing director restricted?

As in the case of a director of an AG, the powers of a managing director may be subject to statutory and contractual restrictions. As the appointment of a managing director of a GmbH is usually made by the shareholders, his powers may be restricted not only by the articles of association and/or a service agreement, but also by separate decisions of the shareholders. In contrast to a stock corporation, the shareholders' instructions may concern the day-to-day business of the company.

What are the statutory restrictions on a managing director's powers?

There are two main statutory restrictions:

- according to s 35 of the GmbH Act and s 181 of the German Civil Code, a managing director may not enter into a commercial contract with the company on his own account or as an agent of third parties, unless the articles or a special resolution specifically authorises such a transaction.
- in addition, matters of principal importance, such as the modification of the articles of association, require a resolution of the shareholders in general meeting.

What are the most usual restrictions on the authority of managing directors of a GmbH?

The powers of a managing director of a GmbH may be restricted further than those of a director of an AG, since the articles of association of a GmbH may provide that certain transactions are subject to shareholder approval, for example property transactions, borrowing, the entering into long-term agreements, participation in other companies, the sale of substantial company assets and contracts with employees of the company of a certain level.

What are the duties of a managing director of a GmbH?

Section 43 of the GmbH Act stipulates that he must act with the diligence of a proper businessperson.

In deciding if a managing director has breached this duty, a court will look at the standards to be expected of businesspeople generally, and it will assess the managing director's professional performance and his fiduciary relationship with the company.

Where a managing director has a special service agreement with the company, he must respect the contractual duties set out in it, in particular the duties of care and competence. If the managing director is also a shareholder, he may have an increased duty of good faith towards the company. This can involve a duty not to compete with the company and the prohibition on the use of business opportunities for his own purposes.

What are the rights of a GmbH against its managing director?

Section 43 of the GmbH Act enables the company to claim damages for the breach of a managing director's duty of diligence by reason of negligence or wilful default. In such cases, the company is represented by its shareholders who have to adopt a resolution to claim the damages.

Can a managing director avoid this liability?
Yes.

- A managing director is not liable if he acted under the direction of the shareholders or the supervisory board, unless it was evident to him that the instruction was null and void for breach of imperative law or unlawful for other reasons.
- The articles of association may modify the responsibility of a managing director, but they may not exclude liability for wilful breach of duty or culpable negligence.

Is there any time bar to claims?
Generally a claim must be brought within five years of the event giving rise to it. However, certain specific breaches of duty by a managing director (being those which constitute a breach of ss 823 *et seq* of the Bürgerliches Gesetzbuch (BGB) (German Civil Code) (tort)) will attract a three-year time limit. The shorter limitation period starts to run at the date when the injured party has knowledge both of the damage and the identity of the party causing the damage. The maximum period within which a claim can be brought is 30 years from the event complained of.

What must the company prove?
It must prove:

- that there has been damage to its interests; and
- that the damage was caused by the conduct of the managing director.

Is there any defence?
Yes, provided the managing director can prove that he worked diligently and according to a binding shareholders' resolution.

Does a managing director of a GmbH undertake any other specific liabilities?
Yes. The following liabilities arise out of the conduct of the business of a GmbH company.

- A managing director is subject to restrictions on own-share acquisition and protection of capital generally (s 43(3) GmbH Act) and is in this context liable *vis-à-vis* the company.
- He could be liable to the company under s 64, para 2 of the GmbHG (GmbH Act) which concerns payments made by the managing director for a company in insolvency.

- A managing director becomes liable if he makes payments out of share capital to shareholders, which result in the reduction of share capital below the legal minimum level. If other shareholders subsequently incur losses in restoring capital to the correct level, the managing director must then reimburse these other shareholders.

What about liability for payment of company taxes and social insurance contributions?

With regard to the payment of company taxes, the managing director of a GmbH has the same liability as a member of the executive board of an AG (see above).

Moreover, the managing directors are responsible for the payment of social security contributions relating to the staff of the company.

What about criminal liability?

- A managing director could incur criminal liability when a company goes bankrupt.
- The GmbH Act creates particular criminal offences, eg omitting to file a petition for bankruptcy when required, failure to notify a declaration stating the loss of more than half the minimum share capital to the shareholders, or the making of a false declaration concerning the full payment of share capital or the reduction of share capital. Criminal liability for breach of the duty of secrecy is provided for in s 85 of the GmbH Act.

Is a company liable for the default of its managing director?

The company itself is liable to third parties for damages resulting from acts of the managing directors committed in the course of their duties.

Do the rules for product liability apply to a managing director as well?

Yes. As a corporation, the GmbH follows the same rules of product liability, and the managing directors are subject to the same liability as a director of an AG.

What are the consequences of company insolvency for a managing director?

As in the case of an AG, a managing director must file an insolvency petition within three weeks of the company's insolvency. The opening of bankruptcy proceedings results in the dissolution of the company.

The bankruptcy of a managing director as an individual does not affect the company and he can remain as managing director in these circumstances.

How can a managing director be dismissed?
A managing director of a GmbH may be dismissed without any reason and at any time, unless:

- his powers of representation result directly from the articles of association;
- there is a special right for the managing director's activity; or
- his appointment is for life.

In these three cases, a managing director can only be dismissed for good cause such as a material breach of duty, misconduct, incapacity to manage the company's affairs etc.

By whom can a managing director be dismissed?
The shareholders have the power to dismiss a managing director, unless the articles provide that the supervisory board, an advisory board or certain shareholders have this power instead. Where the Co-determination Acts apply the supervisory board has the power of dismissal.

Does the termination of a managing director's service agreement affect his appointment as managing director?
If there is a service agreement with a managing director the consequences are the same as with an AG (see above).

May a managing director of a GmbH resign?
A managing director of a GmbH may resign at any time for an important reason. It is uncertain whether or not a resignation may be possible without an important reason. The Supreme Court of Bavaria stated that it is impossible in the case where a limited company has only one shareholder and the shareholder himself is the managing director of a company unless he appoints a new managing director.

A managing director may terminate his service agreement for important reasons on the giving of two weeks' notice. In this context, important reasons may include a conflict of interest, health problems etc. The two-week period does not vary depending on the length of the managing director's service agreement.

What is the position in what was formerly East Germany?
Since the reunification of East and West Germany on 3 October 1990, West German law is in general applicable to the new 'Länder' subject to a number of transitional provisions.

The Limited Liability Companies Act and the Stock Corporation Act became effective by force of law as early as 1 July 1990, as a result of the monetary, economic and social union. Up to the date of reunification on 3 October 1990, it was possible to organise limited liability companies with a share capital of only 20,000 DM. The capital of such companies has to be increased to 50,000 DM by 1 July 1995, if the application for registration in the commercial register was filed before 30 June 1990. If registration is applied for between 1 July and 2 October 1990 the capital has to be increased as early as 1 July 1992.

Enterprises which were previously state-owned have been changed by law into limited liability companies (GmbH), while the bigger economic units which were previously state-owned collective combines have been changed into stock corporations (although in rare cases also into limited liability companies). The shares both in stock corporations and in limited liability companies are held by the 'Treuhandanstalt' in Berlin. Some of the stock corporations themselves hold the shares in enterprises of which they were in charge before reunification. The former state-owned premises and real estates which were used by the enterprises for operational reasons have become property of the companies.

The reunification treaty makes possible the rescission of expropriations of Jewish property made between 1933 and 1945, and of expropriations of property in general from 1949. The provisions governing applications for the retransfer of such enterprises and premises have now expired, although the majority of the filed applications have not yet been reviewed. Retransfers will, however, also be possible after the expiration of the time limit. If the Treuhandanstalt has sold an enterprise, despite justified claims for its retransfer, the purchase contract remains effective but the Treuhandanstalt is liable for damages.

Some major enterprises have been divided into smaller entities which have been sold and transferred, although these transactions might be invalid for legal reasons. Due to a new law which was enacted on 5 April 1991, the potential invalidity of such individual transfers will be cured by way of registration in the commercial register of the enterprises which were formed through division.

Altogether, the situation in the new Länder is very complex, particularly as practice diverges very much from the statutory provisions which are subject to frequent revisions.

GREECE

George Babanikolos

What are the main types of company which exist in Greece?
There are two main categories of company in Greece:

- civil companies, which engage in civil activities, such as buying and selling land, home-leasing, farming etc;
- commercial companies, which engage in commercial enterprises and activities. Commercial companies are divided into 'personal' and 'capital' companies.

PERSONAL COMPANIES

There are four different forms of personal company:

- general partnerships;
- limited partnerships;
- silent partnerships;
- joint ventures.

What is a general partnership ('Omorrythmos Etairia')?
This can be recognised by the letters 'OE' after the company's name and is defined (Article 20, Commercial Law) as a contract between two or more persons with the object of acting together commercially under a firm name.

All partners have joint, several and unlimited liability for the partnership debts. The name of at least one partner must be included in the name of the company.

The partnership agreement must be published in the Books of Companies of the Court of First Instance of the district in which the partnership has its seat. The OE obtains legal personality once the partnership agreement has been published.

Management of the OE
The OE does not have a board of directors. It is managed by a business-manager ('diachiristis') who may be a partner or a third party. The

management may be provided for by the partnership agreement, otherwise all the partners are responsible for the management of the OE

Liability of partners
The partnership as a legal entity is liable for its commitments and debts, although the partners are also liable, jointly and severally, to the extent of their personal property, for the partnership's obligations. The same is true for the business-manager, who is liable to the extent of all his or her personal property, even if he or she is a third party and not a partner.

What is a limited partnership ('Eterorrythmos Etairia')?

This can be recognised by the letters 'EE' after the company's name and is defined (Article 23, Commercial Law) as a contract between a) one or more partners ('omorrythmos etairos'), who are individually liable without limitation for the partnership debts and obligations and b) one or more partners who are liable to the extent of their contribution to the partnership ('eterorrythmos etairos'). The partnership agreement must be published in the Books of Companies of the Court of First Instance of the district in which the company has its seat. Once again, the company obtains legal personality after the publication of the partnership agreement.

Management of the EE
Only the general partner can engage in the management of the EE.

Liability of partners
The liability and powers of the general partner in the EE are similar to those of the general partner in the OE.

What is a silent partnership ('Aphanis' or 'Metochiki Etairia')?

This is defined as a partnership by which the partners agree to co-operate and pursue one or more mercantile activities (Articles 47–50, Commercial Law). However, only one partner appears to carry out all the mercantile business, while the other partner or partners remain 'silent' and have no say in the management of the partnership. The partnership agreement sets out the obligations of the partners. This type of company has no legal personality and is not extensively used.

What is a joint venture ('Koinopraxia')?

Although this type of company is not provided for in the Commercial Law, legal practice defines it as an agreement under which parties co-operate in order to attain a certain objective.

CAPITAL COMPANIES

The main types of capital companies in Greece are:

- companies limited by shares; and
- companies with limited liability.

What is a company limited by shares ('Anonymos Etairia')?

This can be recognised by the letters 'AE' after the name of the company. A company limited by shares is governed by Law 2190/1920, as amended by Legislative Decree 4237/1962, codified by Royal Decree 174/1963 and further codified by Presidential Decrees 409/1986 and 498/1987.

The AE is the purest form of capital company, having a fixed capital divided by shares which are freely transferable. The minimum amount of share capital is 5,000,000 Dr, unless the company issues public shares by subscription, when the share capital must be at least 10,000,000 Dr. Increased amounts of share capital are required for certain types of AE, such as banking companies, insurance companies, leasing companies, and factoring companies (see below).

A company limited by shares must be founded by at least two persons, natural or legal, called shareholders. The minimum contents of the company's statutes, which must be drawn up before a notary public (Article 40, Commercial Law) are set out in Article 2 of Law 2190/1920, as replaced by Article 2 of Presidential Decree 409/86.

The founders of the company must subscribe to the capital of the company, which must be paid up within two months of the date of publication of the summary of the company's statutes in the Bulletin of Companies of the *Government Gazette*. The statutes are examined by the Ministry of Commerce and, provided they comply with the legal requirements, a decision is issued by the Minister of Commerce. This decision effects the establishment of the AE and the administrative approval of its statutes.

Both the decision and the statutes must be entered in the Register of Companies Limited by Shares, which is kept by the Ministry of Commerce. A summary of this entry, and of the statutes of the company, is published in the Bulletin of Companies of the *Government Gazette*.

The AE is managed by the board of directors (Article 18, para 1, Law 2190/1920), which represents the company in court or extrajudicially. The board is headed by a president, the equivalent of a chairman, and it may appoint one or more persons, who do not have to be members of the board, to represent the company. This person is called the managing director ('Diephthinon Symvoulos').

How many directors must a Greek company have?
The number of directors on the board is fixed by the statutes of the company. The minimum number is three, although there is no upper limit.

Who appoints a director?
The directors are elected by the shareholders in general meeting. However, the following should be noted.

- According to Article 34, Law 2190/1920, the founders of the AE appoint the first board of directors in the statutes of the company.
- The board of directors itself may, if so authorised by the company's statutes, elect directors to replace directors who have resigned, died or otherwise forfeited their duties. Directors elected in this manner hold office until the next shareholders' meeting.
- According to Article 18, para 3, Law 2190/1920, the company's statutes may give to a certain shareholder or shareholders the right to appoint up to one-third of the members of the board of directors. The statutes must determine the conditions governing this right especially in relation to participation in the company's capital and the blocking of the shares. The shareholders who exercise this right do not have the right to participate in the election of the remaining members of the board of directors.

Is there any limitation on the number of directorships which an individual can hold in any number of companies?
There is no limitation on the number of directorships which an individual can hold. Nevertheless, Article 23 Law 2190/1920 provides that members of the board of directors, and any other 'executive directors', may not, without the consent of the shareholders' meeting, do anything for their own or a third party's benefit which falls within the scope of the company's objects, nor may they participate as general partners in partnerships which carry on a similar business to that of the company. 'Executive directors' under Greek law are superior officers of the company, who are employees but not members of the board of directors.

Who can be a director?
A director may be an individual or a corporate body. In the case of a corporate body, all powers and duties of the director are exercised by its

authorised natural representative. The director does not need to be of Greek nationality or a shareholder, unless the company's statutes provide otherwise.

Who is excluded from being a director?
The following people cannot be directors:

- legally incapacitated persons;
- members of parliament;
- civil servants;
- auditors of the company; and
- any person who has gone into bankruptcy or compulsory administration.

What is the relationship between the company and the director?
The relationship between the company and the director is governed by an agreement called 'the mandate', which is regulated by Articles 713–29, Civil Code. The director acts in the name of the company and must protect the company's interests and respect the secrecy of the company's affairs.

How is a director rewarded?
The members of the board of directors may or may not be rewarded by the company. They usually receive payment for their attendance at board meetings. According to Article 24, Law 2190/1920, this remuneration must be paid out of the company's profits and is to be taken out of the balance of the net profits, after the deduction of the amounts contributed to ordinary reserves and the distribution of first dividend.

Any other remuneration must be approved by a specific decision of the shareholders' meeting. If this remuneration is found to be excessive, it may be reduced by the court.

Payments to the directors for services rendered to the company pursuant to a specific agreement do not need to be approved by the shareholders' meeting or the court.

Are there any restrictions on benefits which the director can receive from the company?
Under Article 23A, Law 2190/1920, loans by the company to the original shareholders, members of the board of directors, general managers or managers of the company, family relatives up to the third degree by blood or by marriage, or to their spouses, or the granting of credits and guarantees to such people, are absolutely prohibited.

The same absolute prohibition is applicable to loans or the granting of credits by subsidiary companies or by general partnerships in which the company participates.

What are the tax contributions to be paid by a director?
* The director is not taxed on the payments received for his or her attendance at Board Meetings. The corresponding tax is paid by the AE.
* The remuneration paid to a director for his or her services to the company as an employee is taxed as salary under the general tax provisions.
* Any payments made to the director for his or her services to the board of directors are taxed as income from commercial activities.

What are the social security contributions to be paid by a director?
A director who only receives payments for his or her attendance at board meetings is not obliged to make social security contributions. However, if the director is at the same time an employee of the company, he or she is obliged to pay social security contributions on an amount corresponding to his or her salary.

What is the basis of a director's authority?
A director's authority is derived from the following sources:

* the statutes of the company;
* Law 2190/1920, as amended;
* the decisions of the shareholders' meetings; and
* the decisions of the board of directors.

What are the powers of a director?
Under Articles 18 and 22 of Law 2190/1920, the board of directors represents the company both in court and extrajudicially and has broad authority to decide on any matter related to the management of the company, the administration of its property or the implementation of the company's objectives.

The board of directors acts collectively. However, the law allows representation of the company by one or more directors on specific matters, as well as assignment of the powers of the board, in whole or in part, to one or more directors acting in the name of the company. The company's statutes determine the specific powers of the board of directors.

How are the powers of a director restricted?
* A director must act within the limits of the company's objects. However, acts which exceed the scope of the company's objects bind the

company in relation to third parties, unless it is proved that the third party knew or ought to have known of the violation.

- The fact that the powers of the board of directors have been restricted by a resolution of the general meeting may not be relied on against third parties acting in good faith.
- The directors or managers of the company may not, without the authorisation of the shareholders' meeting, on their own account or on the account of a third party carry out any activity which falls within the scope of the objects of the company or participate as general partners in partnerships which carry on similar business.

In the case of violation of the above prohibition, the company has the right to claim damages from the director. The company may ask for the transaction of the director or the manager to be considered as having been made for the benefit of the company or, in the case of a transaction made on behalf of a third party, to claim the payment received by the director or, alternatively, the assignment of his or her claim to such payment (Article 23, Law 2190/1920).

What are the duties of a director?

- Under the provisions of Article 22a, para 3 of Law 2190/1920, the members of the board of directors must keep strictly confidential any details of the company's affairs which come to their knowledge in their capacity as directors.
- According to Article 23, Law 2190/1920, the members of the board of directors are prohibited from competing with the company.
- All members of the board of directors are liable to the company for any fault committed in the management of the company, in particular for omissions or false entries in the balance sheet which conceal the actual financial condition of the company.

The directors are liable for every fault (fraudulent or negligent), while the managing director must act with utmost diligence.

What are the penalties for a breach of duty by a main board director?

Directors are liable to the company for damage caused due to their management.

The company must bring its claim against a director who is in breach of his or her duty within three years of the date on which the act was committed. However, if the damage was caused by fraud, the claim is barred after ten years.

Violation of the provisions of Article 23, Law 2190/1920, which concern contracts between the company and members of the board of directors or family relatives, renders the offender liable to imprisonment and/or a fine (Article 58a, Law 2190/1920).

Is a company liable for the default of its director?

Civil liability
Article 211, Greek Civil Code provides that the company is liable for the acts and omissions of its legal representatives, ie those directors authorised to represent the company.

Criminal liability
The company, being a legal entity, has no criminal liability. However, the company's legal representatives will be criminally liable for any acts or omissions of the company.

What are the consequences of a company insolvency for directors?
In a company insolvency, Greek law imposes criminal liability on the directors who are specially authorised to represent the company. Imprisonment of at least one year is provided for in the case of a fraudulent insolvency, while in the case of a simple insolvency, the sanction is a maximum of two years' imprisonment. The bankruptcy of the company as a legal entity does not affect the members of the board of directors.

How does an individual cease to be a director?
An individual ceases to be a director for the following reasons:

- When his or her term of office as a director comes to an end. The term of office, which is usually fixed in the company's statutes, may not exceed six years (Article 19, Law 2190/1920), although a director may be re-elected.
- Any time, if his or her office is terminated by the shareholder or shareholders who appointed him or her (Article 18, para 3, Law 2190/1920).
- By decision of the president of the Court of First Instance, upon the demand of shareholders representing at least one-tenth of the paid-up share capital, for serious cause relating to the person of the director (Article 18, para 4, Law 2190/1920).
- A director also loses his or her office in the case of resignation, death, incapacity, bankruptcy or insolvency.

How has the insider dealing directive been implemented in Greece?
Under Law 1806/1988, any person who him or herself, or through any third person, uses secret information relating to the activities of an enterprise for the purpose of acquiring or selling shares in that enterprise through the Stock Exchange, is subject to imprisonment of at least three months and/or a fine.

What is the responsibility of a director for acts or defaults of a company under competition legislation and consumer protection measures?
- Under Greek competition law, the company itself is responsible and not the director. However, if the company violates a court decision issued on a competition matter, the company's legal representatives (as defined above) face imprisonment for up to one year.
- The same is true in relation to consumer protection measures.

What is the scope of product liability in Greece and who is responsible for it?
Criminal liability
Under Greek law, only a member of the board of directors is personally responsible if the company faces liability under the product liability measures. The board of directors must allocate responsibility for product liability to one or more of its members. If no such allocation is made, the president or managing director bears this responsibility.

Civil liability
Both the company and the manager responsible for product liability are liable for any damage caused to consumers by a defective product.

What companies are limited by shares?
Further to Law 2190/1920, as amended by special legislation, the following types of companies limited by shares (AE's) are recognised in Greece:

- banking companies, which are governed by Laws 5076/1931, 1665/1951, 2292/1952, Legislative Decree 588/1948 and the basic Law 2190/1920;
- insurance companies, which are governed by Legislative Decree 400/1970 and Laws 1380/1983 and 2190/1920;
- investment-portfolio companies and mutual funds, which are governed by Legislative Decree 608/1970 and Law 2190/1920;

- stock exchange companies limited by shares, which are governed by Law 1806/1988;
- football companies limited by shares which are governed by Law 879/1979;
- leasing companies limited by shares which are governed by Law 1665/1986;
- factoring companies, which are governed by Law 1905/1990;
- maritime companies, which are governed by Law 959/1979;
- venture capital and small business-financing companies, which are governed by Law 1775/1988;
- co-operatives ('Synetairismos'), which are governed by Law 1667/1986. In particular, agricultural co-operatives are governed by Law 921/1979, while co-operatives established by municipalities and communities are governed by Presidential Decree 80/1986.

What is a company with limited liability ('Etairia Periorismenis Efthinis')

This can be recognised by the letters E π E. (pronounced EPE) after the name of the company. This type of company, which is governed by Law 3190/1955, as amended by Presidential Decree 419/1986, is chosen for small and medium-sized companies. The 'limited liability' refers to the liability of the members of the company (who are called partners rather than shareholders) while the company itself, as a legal entity, is liable without limit for its corporate obligations and debts.

The EPE requires a small share capital of at least 200,000 Dr for its constitution. The EPE must be formed by two or more persons, natural or legal, who are called partners or members.

A copy of the company's statutes, which must be drawn up before a notary public, must be filed with the Clerk of the Court of First Instance of the district where the company has its seat. A summary of the statutes of the company must be published in the Bulletin of Companies of the *Government Gazette*.

The EPE is not managed by a board of directors, but by one or more business-managers ('Diachiristis'). The manager of the EPE may be appointed by the statutes of the company or by resolution of the members' meeting.

The manager is not required to be a member of the company and he or she may be a natural or legal person. Civil servants and university professors are prohibited from being managers and members of an EPE. In the absence of any provision in the statutes of the company, the management of the EPE belongs to all the members of the company, who act collectively. There is no limitation on the number of companies with limited liability of which an individual may be business-manager.

How is the manager of an EPE rewarded?
The statutes of the company or, if they are silent on this question, the partners' meeting, determine the remuneration of the business-manager which is regarded as a salary for his or her services as manager.

Are there any restrictions on the benefits which the business-manager of an EPE can receive from the company?
The company's statutes may impose restrictions on such benefits. In addition, under Article 32, Law 3190/1955, if the manager is a partner of the company, he or she is prohibited from giving loans to the company secured by a direct lien on the company's property.

What are the tax contributions to be paid by a manager?
A manager is taxed in the commercial income category. The rate and method of taxation are provided for under the relevant tax legislation.

What are the social security contributions to be paid by a manager?
It depends on whether or not the manager is a partner of the company.

If the manager is, he or she contributes as a merchant, whereas if the manager is not a partner, he or she is subject to the social security contributions paid by employees.

What is the basis of a manager's authority?
The business-manager derives his or her authority from the following sources:

- the statutes of the company;
- Articles 17, 21 and 25 of Law 3190/1955;
- the partners' meeting.

What are the powers of a manager?
A manager is entitled to represent the company and may bind it by his or her signature under the company's seal or in the firm's name.

How are the powers of a manager restricted?
- The manager has extensive powers to act within the scope of the company's business. However, any act of the manager which exceeds the company's objects is binding on the company in relation to third parties, unless the company proves that the third party knew or ought to

have known that this particular act was outside the scope of the company's objects.

- The statutes may limit the manager's powers.
- The manager is prohibited from competing with the company (Article 20, Law 3190/1955).

What are the duties of a manager?

- The manager must keep the company's affairs secret.
- The manager is obliged to keep, in Greek, the commercial and tax books required by the tax legislation, as well as a book of members of the company, a book of minutes of the meetings and a book of minutes of management (Article 25, Law 3190/1955).

What are the penalties for a breach of duty by a manager?

- The manager is liable to the company, to the partners and to any third party for damage resulting from any infringement of the law governing a company with limited liability, or from a breach of the company's statutes or for damage caused by mismanagement (Article 26, Law 3190/1955). Claims against the manager are barred after five years (Article 26, para 3, Law 3190).
- Under Article 351, Penal Law, managers are liable to up to one year's imprisonment and/or a fine for violation of the business secrecy rules.
- Managers are personally liable for the tax obligations of the company.

Is a company liable for the default of its manager?
Yes.

What are the consequences of a company insolvency for a manager?
In a company insolvency, the business-manager of an EPE is subject to the same liability as the director of an AE (see above).

What are the consequences of a company bankruptcy for a manager?
The bankruptcy of an EPE does not extend to the manager and/or the partners of the company.

How does an individual cease to be a manager?
An individual ceases to be a manager upon the termination of his or her office by resignation or by revocation. In the case of revocation, it depends on whether the manager is a member of the company or a third party, as follows.

1 If the manager is a member of the company and was appointed by the company's statutes for a definite period, his or her office can only be revoked before the end of that period for a serious reason and only, after a resolution of the partners' meeting, by a court decision (Article 19, Law 3190/1955). If the manager was appointed for an indefinite period, his or her office may be revoked by a resolution of the partners' meeting.
2 If a third party was appointed as manager, his or her office may be revoked at any time by a resolution of the partners' meeting. The revoked manager may have a claim for damages against the EPE (Article 19, Law 3190/1955).

In both cases (1) and (2), this resolution must be published in accordance with Article 8, Law 3190/1955.

What is the responsibility of a director for acts or defaults of a company with limited liability under competition legislation and consumer protection measures?
The rules applicable to a company limited by shares (see above) also apply to a company with limited liability.

What is the scope of product liability in Greece and the responsibility of the manager of an EPE?
The general rules on criminal and civil liability for defective products applicable to a company limited by shares (see above) also apply, *mutatis mutandis*, to a company with limited liability.

IRELAND

James O'Dwyer, Siobhan Downey

The most important enactment affecting companies in the Republic of Ireland was the Companies Act 1963. Since then, there have been a number of legislative enactments which have yet to be consolidated into one Act.
These are as follows:

- the European Communities (Company) Regulations 1973, implementing the first EC directive on company law;
- the Companies (Amendment) Act 1977;
- the Companies (Amendment) Act 1982;
- the Companies (Amendment) Act 1983, implementing the second EC directive on company law;
- the European Communities (Stock Exchange) Regulations 1984, implementing the EC admissions directive (No 79/279), the EC listing particulars directive (No 80/390) and the EC interim reports directive (No 82/121);
- the Companies (Amendment) Act 1986, implementing the fourth EC directive on company law;
- the Companies (Amendment) Act 1990; and
- the Companies Act 1990.

What are the main types of company which exist in Ireland?
The two main types of companies which exist in Ireland are:

the private limited company;
the public limited company ('plc').

What is a private limited company?
The characteristics of a private company are defined in s 33 of the 1963 Act as a company with a share capital and having articles of association which:

- restrict the right to transfer shares;
- limit the number of members to 50; and
- prohibit any invitation to the public to subscribe for shares or debentures.

A private company must always have a minimum of two shareholders and must (unless granted a licence by the Minister for Industry and Commerce enabling the company to omit them) put the words 'Limited', or the abbreviation 'Ltd' or the Irish equivalents 'Teoranta' or 'Teo' at the end of its name.

What is a public limited company?

A public limited company is not defined by statute, but may be defined as any registered limited company which is not private and must have a minimum of seven shareholders. It must put the words 'Public Limited Company', 'plc' or the Irish equivalent at the end of the name. The 1983 Act provides that every plc must have a minimum authorised share capital of at least IR£30,000, of which 25 per cent of the nominal value of each share and the whole of any premium on each share must be paid up.

While a private company's articles must have a restriction in relation to the transfer of shares, such a requirement does not apply to a plc. If a plc's shares are to be traded on the Stock Exchange, it must have a provision in its articles which enables the free transfer of shares.

How are private and public companies incorporated?

A number of documents must be delivered to the Registrar of Companies in order to register a company in Ireland. The documents to be delivered to register a private company are:

- the memorandum of association ('memorandum');
- the articles of association ('articles');
- a Companies Office Form A1 which, *inter alia*, requires certain particulars of the first directors, the secretary or joint secretaries of the company, the situation of the company's registered office and a capital duty statement in accordance with the Finance Act 1973 (capital duty is assessed at the rate of 1 per cent on the assets contributed (including cash) for shares allotted);
- a statutory declaration, made by a solicitor engaged in the registration of the company or by one of the persons named as a first director or secretary of the company, certifying that all of the requirements necessary for the registration of the company have been complied with;
- a bank draft for the appropriate registration fee.

Following receipt of these documents, the Registrar of Companies will issue a certificate of incorporation indicating the right of the company to commence business.

Where the company is to be registered as a plc, an additional statutory declaration must be delivered to the Registrar of Companies, made by a director or secretary of the company and confirming:

- that the nominal value of the company's allotted share capital is not less than the authorised minimum (ie not less than IR£30,000);
- the amount paid up at the time of application on the allotted share capital of the company;
- the amount or estimated amount of the preliminary expenses of the company and the person to whom any of those expenses have been paid or are payable; and
- any amount or benefit paid or given or intended to be paid or given to any promoter of the company and the consideration for the payment or benefit.

Must companies be limited by shares?

Irish companies may be registered with either limited or unlimited liability. A limited liability company may be limited by shares or by guarantee.

Limited by shares

A member of a company limited by shares must pay to the company the full nominal amount of each share the company has issued to such member. Subject to this, the member has no further liability in excess of that amount if the company subsequently goes into liquidation.

Thus, the member's liability to the company is limited to the amount unpaid or outstanding on the member's shares.

Limited by guarantee

A company may be limited by guarantee, but s 7 of the 1983 Act prohibits the formation of a public company which is limited by guarantee and has a share capital. The members of a company limited by guarantee undertake to contribute a specified amount in the event of the company being wound up. Companies limited by guarantee are usually non-profit-making organisations.

Unlimited company

A company may be registered with unlimited liability, in which case its members are jointly and severally liable to pay in full all of the company's debts if the company is wound up. Unlimited liability companies are more common nowadays in Ireland as a) the rules on capital maintenance do not apply to such companies and, accordingly, capital may be returned to its members; b) the obligation to file copies of annual accounts does not apply to unlimited companies due to an exemption contained in the 1986 Act; and

c) the 1 per cent capital duty is not payable on the allotment of shares in unlimited companies. In addition, the provisions of the fourth EC directive relating to company accounts do not apply to companies with unlimited liability.

Are shares of all public companies traded on a stock exchange?

The shares in a plc may, but need not be, traded on a stock exchange, but to have its shares traded on the Irish Stock Exchange, a company must comply with the regulations in the '*Yellow Book*' (the Admission of Securities to Listing) or the other regulations of the Irish Stock Exchange relating to shares which are not listed but which are dealt in on one of the 'subsidiary' markets.

What are the requirements for the management structure of public and private companies?

A company must have at least two directors and the articles normally set out the maximum number of directors. The articles of association of companies vest certain powers in the directors and certain other powers are reserved to the shareholders. Usually the articles provide for the day-to-day management to be undertaken by the board of directors (as is provided by reg 80 of Part I of Table A to the 1963 Act, which is a set of 'model' articles which a company may adopt, with or without modification). The board of the company usually appoints a chairperson and may appoint a managing director. There is still no draft legislation to implement the twelfth EC Directive on single member companies, which should be made effective by 1/1/92.

How is a chairperson appointed?

A chairperson is usually appointed by the board of directors and generally presides at every shareholders' meeting of the company. If no such chairperson is appointed, or if he or she is not present at the meeting in question, the directors are entitled to appoint one of the directors present to act as chairperson. In certain circumstances the members of the company may appoint one of the members to act as chairperson.

How is the managing director appointed?

The articles of association normally provide that the directors may appoint one of their number as managing director for such period and with such powers as they think fit. The terms and conditions of his or her employment and removal are set out either in his or her contract of employment or in the articles. The directors are entitled to terminate the appointment, but, in addition, if the shareholders remove the managing director from office as director (which they may do by ordinary resolution), then he or she automatically ceases to be managing director.

Can shareholders be directors?
A shareholder may be a director of the company, but must not confuse his or her role as a director with his or her expectations as a shareholder when making managerial decisions.

Do shareholders have the right to control the day-to-day running of a company?
The articles of association usually provide that the day-to-day management is vested in the board of directors. However, under the terms of shareholders' agreements in private companies, certain rights and thereby some control are sometimes reserved to the shareholders. Shareholders have the right to dismiss directors by the passing of an ordinary resolution in a shareholders' meeting (s 182 of the 1963 Act and reg 99 of Part I of Table A).

How is the board of directors made up?
The board of directors is usually composed of executive directors and non-executive directors. Executive directors have an executive function in the day-to-day management of the company and are employees of the company. Non-executive directors are not employed by the company and are not involved on a daily basis with the running of the company's business.

What are the articles of association of a company?
Articles of association must be filed with the Registrar of Companies on the incorporation of a company. The articles set out the rules governing the internal management of the company's affairs, certain rights and obligations of shareholders and directors, and the procedures to be followed in relation to shareholders' meetings, directors' meetings, and transfer and transmission of shares. The 1963 Act contains model sets of articles for different types of companies.

What is the memorandum of association of a company?
A memorandum of association must be filed with the Registrar of Companies on incorporation. A memorandum of association, in accordance with s 6(1) of the 1963 Act, must contain the following:

- the name of the company;
- the objects of the company;
- a statement that the company is to have limited liability (if this is the case);
- the authorised share capital; and
- the subscribers' wish to be associated as a company.

Do the directors have total control with regard to the running of a company?

In general, the directors have total control subject to duties of care and good faith to the company. Directors may delegate some of their powers to a managing director or to a committee of the board. Certain fundamental decisions, such as a change of the company's name, alteration of its memorandum or articles of association, and increase of the authorised share capital, may be taken only by the passing of an appropriate resolution by a shareholders' meeting.

What about the annual general meeting (AGM)?

Section 131 of the 1963 Act and reg 48 of Part I of Table A require every company, in each year, to hold an annual general meeting not more than 15 months after the preceding AGM. However, the first AGM may be held at any time within the 18-month period after its incorporation. The directors of the company are obliged to convene the AGM, but, in accordance with s 131(3), if they do not, the Minister for Industry and Commerce may convene it on the application of any member of the company. The ordinary business dealt with at the AGM is outlined in reg 53 of Part I of Table A as:

- to declare a dividend, if any;
- to consider the company's audited profit and loss account and balance sheet, and the accompanying directors' and auditors' reports thereon (copies to be sent to shareholders with the notice, 21 days beforehand);
- to elect directors in place of those retiring; and
- to appoint the company's auditors and fix their remuneration.

Other business may be transacted at the AGM and, in accordance with reg 51 of Part I of Table A, the general nature of such special business must be specified in the notice of the AGM. However, it is more likely that such business would be dealt with at an extraordinary general meeting.

Who may appoint the directors?

Both the shareholders and the directors may appoint directors. The first directors, unless named in the articles of association, are determined by the subscribers to the memorandum. Generally, articles provide that a specified proportion (usually one-third) of the directors should retire at the AGM each year. Directors so retiring are eligible for re-election. This provision is not a legal requirement and is more commonly found in the articles of association of plcs.

The shareholders may appoint an additional director at any shareholders' meeting (including the AGM), provided that sufficient notice has been given. Further, the shareholders may increase or reduce the maximum number of directors by resolution at a shareholders' meeting.

Under reg 98 of Part I of Table A, the directors may appoint anyone as a director, either to fill a casual vacancy on the board or as an additional director. Any director so appointed holds office only until the next AGM and is then eligible for re-election but will not be taken into account to determine the directors who retire by rotation at that meeting.

The articles may include or exclude provisions to the effect outlined above. In private companies, especially joint venture companies, the articles may provide that particular people (eg the parties to a joint venture) may appoint and remove a specified numbers of directors, usually by way of a written notice on the company.

Who can be a director?
Any natural person may be a director, thus a body corporate may not be a director. There are no qualifications necessary, unless the articles provide for a shareholding qualification or some other requirement. There are, however, a number of persons excluded from acting as directors (see below).

Is there any limitation on the number of directorships which the individual can hold in any number of companies?
There is no statutory restriction or limitation on the number of directorships which an individual may hold. However, the articles or a service contract between the company and its director may provide limitations or restrictions (eg that the person in question may become a director of other companies only after obtaining the consent of the first company).

Who is excluded from being a director?
In accordance with the provisions of the Companies Acts and the model articles in Part 1 of Table A, certain persons are prohibited from acting as directors. Under the 1963 Act the persons so prohibited include:

• a body corporate;

- the auditor of a company (or of its holding company or any of its subsidiaries);
- any person who has not obtained the appropriate share qualification in accordance with the company's articles of association (if they require such a qualification) within a period of two months after his or her appointment;
- an undischarged bankrupt;
- a person convicted of an offence in connection with the formation, promotion or management of a company or of any offence involving fraud.

The 1990 Act requires that if a company is unable to pay its debts and is in liquidation or receivership, the court will make a declaration preventing each director of that company from acting as a director of any other company unless certain requirements relating to the capitalisation of that other company are met. Section 150 of the 1990 Act provides that the restriction will not be imposed if the court is satisfied that the individual acted honestly and responsibly or was nominated by a financial institution or a venture capital company to the board of directors of the insolvent company.

In addition, the 1990 Act empowers the courts to make a disqualification order against an auditor, director or other officer, receiver, liquidator or examiner preventing that person from acting in any of those capacities. The normal period of disqualification is five years but, if a disqualification order is breached, the court may increase this period to ten years or such length of time as the court sees fit. The 1990 Act provides for a wide range of circumstances under which a person may be made the subject of a disqualification order, including where the person has been found guilty of fraud or dishonesty, or breach of duty.

There is no restriction in the Act on minors (ie those below the age of 18) being directors, provided they have the necessary capacity. Similarly, there is nothing to stop those in prison being directors, although they may be disqualified if they have been convicted of any of the offences listed above or under the articles of association of the company (see above), or if it means they are absent from board meetings for six months without the board's authority.

What is the relationship between a company and a director?
The relationship varies according to whether the director is an executive director or non-executive director. An executive director is (usually) an employee of the company and is subject to the terms of any service contract

he or she may have and/or to the directions of the board. The fundamental duties of any director (including executive directors) are to act in good faith in the interests of the company and to disregard any personal interests he or she may have (whether as a shareholder, or because he or she has an interest in a contract with the company, or for any other reason).

What is an alternate director?

An alternate director is a proxy or substitute director appointed by a director in accordance with the articles to attend directors' meetings and act as director on his or her behalf. The appointment may be revoked only in accordance with the articles.

There is no difference between an alternate and a substitute director, but it should be noted that in addition to the right to appoint an alternate (if permitted by the articles), a director may assign his or her office to another person under s 199 of the 1963 Act, subject to the approval of special resolution of the shareholders. The assignee takes over all the duties of the assignor who ceases to hold office from the date of the assignment.

What is the position of a shadow director?

The 1990 Act defines a shadow director as a person on whose directions or instructions the directors of the company are accustomed to act, unless advice is merely given in a professional capacity.

This Act extends some provisions of the 1963 Act (for example, in relation to disclosure of interests in contracts with the company) to shadow directors.

How is a director rewarded?

A director is not legally entitled to any remuneration for acting as a director, unless the articles so provide.

Any remuneration paid to a director as an employee is distinct from any remuneration to which he or she may be entitled as a director.

Under s 185 of the 1963 Act, any remuneration paid to a director must be subject to income tax. Further, the aggregate of directors' emoluments must be stated in the annual accounts presented to the members at the AGM.

The articles normally provide that directors are to be paid either the amount determined by a shareholders' meeting or a fixed sum specified in the articles. Fees vary greatly, depending on the type of company involved.

A director is not legally entitled to be paid a pension but the articles may authorise payment of a pension to any director or dependant of the director.

A lump sum payment may be made to a director for loss of office, but the 1963 Act requires that this must be disclosed to the shareholders and approved by them in general meeting.

Most payments made to directors (in their capacity as directors, as distinct from employees) must be approved by the shareholders in general meeting. A properly approved payment will be set aside only if it amounts to:

- a disguised repayment of capital;
- a fraud on the minority; or
- oppression in accordance with s 205 of the 1963 Act.

Are there any restrictions on the benefits which a director may receive from a company?

The 1990 Act contains various restrictions including provisions dealing with fixed-term contracts of directors, substantial property transactions, share option contracts and loans, quasi loans and credit transactions. These are similar to restrictions under UK legislation. The Act requires directors to disclose interests in various contracts. In addition they would be liable to compensate the company for any loss which the company may suffer as a result of a relevant transaction and to account to the company for any gain which the directors may have made in relation to such transactions.

What is the basis of a director's authority?

Shareholders, as owners, control the company and are entitled to manage it, but they delegate management authority to the directors through the articles and directions or resolutions in general or AGMs. However, no such direction will invalidate any prior act of the directors which would have been valid if the direction had not been given.

May the board delegate its powers?

The board may delegate its powers to a managing director and/or to a committee (or committees) of the board, but only in accordance with the articles.

May only a specified number of directors pass valid board resolutions?

The articles govern board meeting procedure.

Subject to this, a simple majority of directors present in person or by alternate is normally sufficient to pass a valid board resolution.

What is the authority of the directors?
Besides the authority given by the articles and decisions made by the shareholders, directors may be granted specific powers under the terms of their service contracts. Thus, if directors have the power to deal with the assets of the company, they must take account of the limitations of the company's objects as set out in the memorandum. Additionally, in carrying out their powers they must exercise the duties of care and good faith which they owe to the company.

What if a director acts outside his or her authority?
Any contract entered into by a director outside his or her authority may be enforced by the other party to the contract provided the other party acted in good faith. However, the company is entitled to seek compensation for any loss suffered by it against the director who exceeded his or her authority.

How are decisions of the board taken?
Usually decisions of the board are taken in accordance with the articles either by a) a resolution of a duly convened meeting of the board, passed by simple majority or b) a written resolution signed by all the directors. The articles may provide that a resolution must be passed by a greater majority and/or that the chairman has a second or casting vote at board meetings.

How can a director be removed from office?
- By a shareholders' resolution in general meeting with special notice.
- By a person specially appointed under the articles. This is useful in joint venture situations.

Has a director any remedy against removal from the board of directors?
A director removed by resolution of the shareholders may have a claim against the company for damages for breach of contract, if he or she is employed by the company. The director also has the following remedies:

- he or she may apply to the High Court for an order to wind-up the company on the grounds that it is just and equitable to do so, on the basis that the removal of the director constitutes a breach of an understanding or agreement between the original members of the company;

- case-law suggests that if he or she is also a shareholder he or she may apply to the High Court for a remedy on the grounds that the affairs of the company are being conducted in a manner oppressive to him or her or in disregard of his or her interests as a member;
- he or she may claim under the Unfair Dismissals Act 1977 and seek compensation, reinstatement or re-engagement;
- he or she may apply to the High Court for relief on the grounds that the relevant fair procedures required for dismissal were not adopted by the company.

What are the principal general duties of a director?

A director must exercise the appropriate skill and care which could reasonably be expected of a person of his or her particular knowledge and experience, must exercise his or her duties in good faith and for proper purposes, and must not place him or herself in a situation whereby his or her personal interests conflict with the interests of the company of which he or she is a director.

What duties of skill and care are required of directors?

Under the 1990 Act, a director may be liable for reckless trading if he or she was a party to the carrying on of any business of the company in a reckless manner, for example:

- where, having regard to the general knowledge, skill and experience that may reasonably be expected of a person in the director's position, he or she ought to have known that his or her actions, or those of the company, would cause loss to creditors of the company; and
- where the company incurred a debt and the director did not honestly believe on reasonable grounds that the company would be able to pay that debt and all its other debts as and when they fell due.

What are the fiduciary duties of a director?

The principal fiduciary duties of a director may be summarised as:

- to act in good faith and in the interests of the company (this is a subjective test);
- to act for proper purposes only, for example not to defeat the wishes of the majority of shareholders;
- to avoid a conflict between the director's duties and his or her own personal interests;
- not to make personal profits from his or her office.

Are there any other statutory duties placed on directors?

Yes, in addition to duties which are generally repeated in the articles of association (such as keeping minutes, having accounts audited and convening the AGM) or are administrative (such as filing returns), the 1990 Act imposes specific restrictions against directors entering into the following, unless certain requirements are met:

- fixed-term contracts of employment for periods in excess of five years between companies and directors;
- substantial property transactions above a certain amount involving a company and a director;
- loans, quasi loans, credit transactions and security arrangements from the company in favour of directors.

The 1990 Act also prohibits dealings by directors in certain options over shares or debentures of the company.

Irish tax legislation requires directors to ensure that the company completes its tax returns, files them and pays the appropriate tax when due.

Is a company liable for the default of its directors?

Any wrong committed by a director in the course of his or her performance of his or her duties as a director may render the company liable for the director's default. This will depend on whether or not the wrong was committed by the director in the course of acting within his or her powers and authorities or otherwise in accordance with instructions given to him or her by the board.

Contracts entered into by a director which have the effect of binding a company, and which are beyond the capacity of the company, may be enforced by the third party against the company if the third party was not actually aware of the company's lack of capacity, and the contract is lawful. Alternatively, if the third party can prove that he or she acted in good faith, it may be possible for the third party to have the contract enforced.

What are the consequences of a company insolvency for its directors?

Directors may be held personally liable for all or part of the debts of the company if they were knowingly a party to the carrying on of any business of the company in a fraudulent or reckless manner.

Additionally, disqualification and restriction orders may be made against directors of insolvent companies in certain circumstances. These provisions also apply to shadow directors.

How does an individual cease to be a director?
An individual ceases to be a director:

- if he or she is holding office for a fixed term, on the expiry of that term;
- if directors are required by the articles of association to retire by rotation at the AGM and, on his or her retirement, the director is not re-elected;
- if he or she is removed from office as a director;
- if he or she resigns;
- in other circumstances, if any, specified by the articles as those in which a director automatically ceases to hold office, and generally these include

  — if he or she becomes of unsound mind,
  — if he or she commits an indictable offence (other than certain exceptions listed in s 184 of the 1963 Act),
  — if he or she has been absent from board meetings without the permission of the board for more than six months;

- if he or she is disqualified or restricted by order of the court from acting as a director; or
- if he or she fails to obtain any necessary shareholding qualification within two months after having become a director, or if he or she ceases to hold the qualification.

May the wrongs of directors be ratified by the members of the company in general meeting?
When directors have breached their duties to the company, an action may be brought against them by the company itself, by the company's liquidator or by an individual shareholder.

The shareholders may, by a majority vote, ratify the wrongs of directors of the company in certain circumstances, thereby absolving those directors of liability to the company. Additionally, any shareholder who is also a director may vote at a shareholders' meeting to absolve him or herself of liability as a director of the company.

There are, however, certain limits on ratification, as follows.

Fraud
Any fraud committed by the directors in connection with company property cannot be ratified by the members.

Fiduciary duties
Where there is a conflict of interests, a director may be held liable to account to the company for personal profits.

Duty of skill and care
A director's negligence and, therefore, his or her breach of duty of skill and care, could be forgiven by the company in general meeting which could vote (by a simple majority) not to bring proceedings against such director, despite any demands of the minority shareholders that such proceedings be brought. An individual who suffers loss as a result of a director's breach of duty cannot bring an action against that individual director, but can, in certain circumstances, bring an action against the company. The company has the right to be indemnified by the director for losses or damage incurred by the company as a result of claims resulting from unratified wrongs.

Bona fide and for a proper purpose
If the directors fail to exercise their fiduciary duties in good faith (bona fide) then any improper action involved is not ratifiable. However, if they act bona fide but for an improper purpose, it is possible for the majority in general meeting to ratify that act.

How are the powers of a director restricted?
The powers of a director are restricted by:

- the provisions of the Companies Acts 1963 to 1990;
- the memorandum and/or articles of association;
- any applicable provisions of a shareholders' agreement to which the director is a party;
- the provisions of a service contract; or
- resolution of the board.

May a director be made personally liable for the acts or defaults of the company under national environmental legislation?
Yes. Environmental legislation in Ireland has become increasingly onerous over the last decade, both in terms of its extent and the penalties for breach.

Significantly, in certain instances where an offence is committed by a company or a person acting on behalf of a company and is proved to have been committed with the consent, connivance or approval of, or to have been facilitated by any neglect on the part of any director, manager, secretary or other official of that company, then that individual will also be guilty of an offence.

The Air Pollution Act 1987 imposes penalties for offences, on summary conviction, of a fine not exceeding IR£1000, or a term of imprisonment not exceeding six months, or both, and, on conviction on indictment, of a fine not exceeding IR£10,000 or imprisonment for any term not exceeding two years, or both. In addition this Act provides for fines for every day on which the offence is continued.

Other areas under national environmental legislation where a director may be made personally liable for an offence are in relation to dangerous substances (the Dangerous Substances Act 1972) and water pollution (the Local Government (Water Pollution) Act 1977). This latter Act, as amended by the Local Government (Water Pollution) (Amendment) Act 1990, goes further in that it enables injured third parties who have suffered loss to make a claim for damages in a civil action and such a claim, by virtue of s 23 of the 1990 Act, could be brought against a director personally.

Are there other areas of domestic legislation under which directors may be made liable for acts or defaults of the company?

The Consumer Information Act 1978 makes it an offence, *inter alia*, to supply false and misleading information in connection with goods and services provided in the course of trade. A director may be guilty if it is proved that an offence was committed with his or her consent or connivance or is attributable to him or her by reason of his or her neglect, or the neglect of any person acting on his or her behalf, even if the director proves that the commission of the offence is due to a mistake or reliance by him or her on information supplied by another person or that he or she took all reasonable precautions and exercised all due diligence. If found guilty the director may be liable to a fine of up to IR£10,000, or a term of imprisonment of up to two years, or both if convicted on indictment.

The Sale of Goods and Supply of Services Act 1980 contains a similar provision in that, under s 6, a director may be made liable where an offence under that Act is committed by the company if the offence is proved to have been committed with his or her consent or connivance or to have been attributable to any neglect on his or her part. If found guilty of such an offence a director may be liable to a fine of up to IR£500 or six months' imprisonment, or both, on summary conviction, or to a fine of up to IR£10,000 or two years' imprisonment, or both, on indictment.

Under relevant Irish tax legislation, directors who fail to comply with the requirements as to filing of tax returns and payment of tax payable by the company, or who provide false information to the Revenue Commissioners, are liable to substantial fines.

Under the Mergers, Takeovers and Monopolies (Control) Act 1978, which requires notification and 'clearance' of proposed mergers and takeovers, any director who knowingly and wilfully authorises or permits any contravention of any provision of the Act (examples are notification and provision of information) by a company which is a party to a proposed merger or takeover, is guilty of an offence.

What are the tax and social security contributions to be paid by a director?

Irish taxation legislation is based on the concept of 'residence'. This, combined with an individual's domicile, determines the extent of his or her exposure to Irish taxation.

Where an Irish resident director performs his or her functions in an executive capacity, under a contract of service, he or she is liable to Irish taxation as an employee under the Irish taxation code and will be subject to tax at rates ranging from the standard rate (currently 29 per cent) to the top rate (currently 52 per cent), depending on the level of his or her income.

An Irish resident director who exercises his or her duties in a non-executive capacity, is similarly liable to tax on the 'emoluments' which he or she receives by virtue of his or her office as director and similarly pays tax at either 29, 48 or 52 per cent (rates for the tax year 1991/2), depending on the level of his or her total earnings. Where a director is engaged to perform services as a person in business on his or her own account (for example, an engineer who advises the company in that capacity), he or she will be chargeable to tax on the income arising from the exercise of his or her profession and in relation to the emoluments arising from his or her post as a director of the company.

Under the Irish taxation code, an individual who holds a public office in the State of Ireland is chargeable to tax on the 'emoluments' of that office, regardless of the residence of the individual, subject to any relief available under double taxation agreements. As the office of director of an Irish incorporated company is deemed to be a public office, the emoluments which the director receives as a result of holding that office are subject to Irish taxation.

Expense payments and benefits-in-kind

Expense payments and benefits-in-kind are chargeable to tax as taxable emoluments. Benefits received by directors of corporate bodies, whatever the amount of their emoluments, are subject to tax.

Pay-related social insurance (PRSI)
The Social Welfare Acts in Ireland contain no specific provisions for company directors. Insurability is conditional upon the existence of a contract of service and if no such contract exists a director will be insured as a self-employed contributor. A non-executive director, whose duties are performed solely in his or her capacity as a director, is not an employed contributor, but a self-employed contributor and will pay pay-related social insurance under Class Sl.

Where a director is employed under a contract of service, he will be insurable for pay-related social insurance as an employee under Class Al.

A director who controls a company and has full control over his or her own duties is insurable as a self-employed individual under Class Sl. The level of contributions and earning ceilings in operation are usually subject to change on an annual basis in the Finance Act. Currently, from 6 April 1991, an employee's PRSI Class Al contribution would be 7.75 per cent on income up to IR£18,000 and 2.25 per cent on amounts in excess of IR£18,000.

Under Class Sl (self-employed) a rate of 7.25 per cent is payable on the first IR£18,000 and 2.25 per cent on amounts in excess of IR£18,000.

How has the insider dealing directive been implemented in Ireland?
Section 108 of the 1990 Act prohibits what has been called 'primary' insider dealing. Section 108 prohibits a person who is connected with a company from dealing in shares in that company when he or she is in possession of information that is not generally available but, if it was, would be likely to have a material effect on the price of the shares. A 'connected' person includes an officer of the company or a related company, a shareholder in the company or a related company, or a person occupying a position that would reasonably be expected to give him or her access to price sensitive information.

Section 108 also prohibits 'tippee' or 'secondary' insider dealing. Thus, where a person has received price-sensitive information relating to a company directly or indirectly from another person and is, or ought reasonably to be, aware that the other person is precluded from dealing in that company's shares, he or she will also be precluded from dealing in them.

A person prohibited from dealing may incur civil liability, and be liable to compensate any other party to the transaction, who did not have the information, for any loss which that party has sustained by reason of any difference between the price in that transaction and the likely price if the information had been generally available. He or she may also be liable to account to the company which issued or made available the shares for any profit accruing to the person from dealing in them. Criminal liability may also be imposed on persons found guilty of offences in relation to insider dealing.

What is the scope of product liability in Ireland and who is responsible for it?

The Liability for Defective Products Act 1991, gives effect to the provisions of Directive 85/374/EC of 25 July 1985, more commonly referred to as the product liability directive. The principal objective of the Act is to introduce into Irish law the remedy of damages for negligence based on the principle of strict or no fault liability. This will co-exist with the fault-based system of liability and is therefore intended to supplement existing civil law on product liability in tort and contract.

The provisions of the Act impose liability on the producer of a product for damage caused wholly or partly by a defect in its product. The definition of 'producer' covers not only the manufacturers of the product, but also any person who puts his name, trade mark or other distinguishing feature on the product and any person who imports the product. Liability may, in certain circumstances, be extended to suppliers of the product.

'Product' is defined by the Act to include all moveables, even though incorporated into another product or into an immoveable, but does not include primary agricultural products which have not undergone initial processing.

A defective product is deemed by the Act to be one which fails to provide the safety a person is entitled to expect, taking all the circumstances into account. However, a product cannot be regarded as defective simply because a better product is subsequently put on the market.

Recovery of damages is by definition limited to circumstances whereby death or personal injury occurs or where the loss of, damage to or destruction of any item of property is caused, provided the item of property is of a type intended for private use and was used by the injured party for private use.

The producer can escape liability for the defective product in certain specified circumstances, including where he or she did not put the product into circulation or in a case where the state of scientific and technical knowledge at the time the product was put into circulation was not such as to enable the existence of the defect to be discovered or where the defect is due to compliance by the producer with requirements imposed by the European Community.

The Act provides that the right of action expires three years from the date the action arose or three years from the date when the plaintiff becomes aware of the damage, the defect and the identity of the producer. All rights of action expire ten years from the date the producer put the product on the market, unless proceedings have commenced in the mean time, although the Minister for Industry and Commerce may provide that the legislation be tied in to the Statute of Limitations.

ITALY

Luca Fabbrinni

The basic provisions of Italian company law, including those relating to the responsibilities of directors are set out in the Civil Code 1942, as amended.

What are the main types of company which exist in Italy?
An active commercial company must take one of the following forms:

- società in nome collettivo, broadly analogous to an English general partnership;
- società in accomandita semplice, broadly analogous to an English limited partnership;
- società in accomandita per azioni, similar in many respects to a limited partnership, but with a share capital;
- società per azioni ('SpA'); or
- società a responsabilità limitata ('Srl').

The SpA. and the Srl, both forms of limited liability companies, are the most usual. In each, with few exceptions, the company itself, as opposed to the individual members, is liable for the company's obligations. This note is therefore confined to these two forms.

Are both the SpA and Srl governed by the same rules?
Many provisions are common to both an SpA and an Srl, and where no distinction is made in this chapter it should be assumed that there is no difference in treatment.

What are the main differences between an SpA and an Srl?
The main distinctions are as follows.

- The minimum capital of an SpA is 200 million L, while that of an Srl is 20 million L. In both cases at least three-tenths of the capital must be paid up.
- While the capital of an SpA is divided into shares in the same way as an English limited company, an Srl does not have shares. Instead the

members' interests are represented by proportionate holdings in the corporate capital, expressed in monetary terms and known as 'quotas'.

- There is no distinction between nominal and issued capital, although an SpA (but not an Srl) may, within certain strict limits, own part of its own capital.
- An Srl cannot issue debentures, but an SpA may.
- An SpA must have a college of 'statutory auditors', who are not auditors in the English sense, but rather a type of 'shadow' board of directors with certain supervisory functions, particularly in relation to the company's accounts. An Srl need have statutory auditors only if the capital is 100 million L or more.

Are the formalities for an Srl less onerous?

Yes, and since the formalities involved in the management of an Srl are generally less onerous, this form has become increasingly popular where there are no particular reasons for establishing an SpA. But there are many reasons for choosing the form of an SpA instead of an Srl. In general, the structure of an SpA is more complex and more expensive to maintain, and is thus better suited to large operations. Unlike an Srl, an SpA may issue bonds as a means of raising capital, may be listed on the Italian Stock Exchange, may have partially paid-in corporate capital and may become a holding company. In addition, an SpA is subject to greater regulation and review and, therefore, offers more security to creditors, investors and other third parties. Furthermore, there are some types of activities which, by law, may be carried on only in the form of an SpA, ie, bond issuance and insurance.

What are the requirements for the management structure of these companies?

The day-to-day management of both an SpA and an Srl is entrusted either to a board of directors or to a sole director.

What about the college of statutory auditors?

In addition, as mentioned above, an SpA, and an Srl with a capital in excess of 100 million L, must appoint a college of statutory auditors of between three and five members (plus two alternates). The statutory auditors remain in office for a term of three years and cannot be removed save for just cause, and then only by resolution of the company in general meeting, approved by the court. The statutory auditors, often professional advisers, are supposed to be independent of the day-to-day management of the company, so that they can exercise a general supervisory role.

What are the most important duties of a college of statutory auditors?

The Civil Code summarises their most important duties as follows:

- to supervise the management of the company;
- to monitor compliance with the law and the company's constitutional documents (that is, the deed of incorporation and by-laws);
- to ensure the proper maintenance of the company's accounts;
- to attend board meetings and general meetings;
- to convene the general meeting when the directors fail to do so.

What are the sanctions imposed upon members of the college of auditors for failure to carry out their duties?

The statutory auditors are jointly and severally liable with the directors for acts or omissions of the latter when the injury would not have occurred if the statutory auditors had exercised vigilance in conformity with the duties of their office.

How do auditors differ from directors?

The board of auditors is responsible for ensuring that the board of directors manages the corporation in accordance with the law and the by-laws. They operate as a supervisory body rather than a decision-making body.

Do auditors get paid and, if so, how much and how often?

The remuneration of the statutory auditors is often set out in the articles of incorporation. If not, it is decided at the shareholders' meeting at the time of their appointment for the entire duration of their term of office.

Do fiduciary duties and insider trading laws apply to auditors?

Statutory auditors must exercise a standard of care equal to that required of a 'mandatario'. A 'mandatario' is a kind of fiduciary who must observe the diligence of a 'good paterfamilias' (which is roughly equivalent to the 'reasonable person' standard in the UK).

The Italian Civil Code also states, in Article 1176, that 'In the performance of obligations inherent in the exercise of a professional activity, diligence shall be evaluated with respect to that activity.' Moreover, if the statutory auditor can be construed as rendering professional services, Article 2236 states that, 'if the professional services involve the solution of technical problems of particular difficulty, the person who renders such services is not liable for damages, except in case of fraud, malice or gross negligence'.

How many directors does a company have?

The company's constitutional documents provide for either a sole director or a board of directors. They specify the size of the board either as a fixed number of directors or by way of a maximum and a minimum. If only a maximum and minimum are laid down, the actual number within those limits is set by the general meeting of shareholders.

Who can be a director?

Directors must be individuals (ie not companies) of full age and capacity.

Should the director be a member of the company?

In the case of an SpA the Civil Code expressly provides that a director need not also be a member of the company. Conversely, a director of an Srl must be a member, unless the constitutional documents say otherwise. In the case of certain particular types of company, such as trustee companies and management companies of common investment funds, additional qualifications are imposed.

Can foreigners be directors?

There is no nationality or residence requirement for directors.

Who is excluded from being a director?

The following categories of persons are excluded:

- persons declared incapable by reason of mental infirmity, alcoholism, drug addiction or certain other causes;
- bankrupts;
- persons on whom certain criminal penalties have been imposed;
- minors.

What can be done about 'delinquent' directors?

Delinquent directors can be removed by vote at a shareholders' meeting. If removal of a director is without just cause, however, the director is entitled to compensation for damages.

Who appoints the directors?

The first directors are named in the constitutional documents, and thereafter the power to appoint directors rests with the general meeting.

What about vacancies?

If for some reason during a corporate year vacancies on the board arise, these must be filled by the remaining directors, with the approval of the college of statutory auditors. Directors so appointed remain in office until the next general meeting. However, if the vacancies to be filled represent more than half of the required number of directors, those still in office must call a special general meeting to nominate replacements. In the absence of all directors the college of statutory auditors must convene the general meeting urgently in order to make appointments.

Does any other body have any right to appoint directors or statutory auditors?

Yes, in the case of SpAs in which the state has a holding or where a special law makes appropriate provision, the company's constitution may confer on the state or on a public body the right to nominate one or more directors or statutory auditors.

What is the relationship between a company and a director?

- The directors are officers of the company. Although appointed by the members, they are not mere delegates, as their powers and duties, deriving from the law and the company's constitution, are inherent to their office.
- Directors may, in certain circumstances, be employees engaged under a service contract.

Is a director ever precluded from being an employee?

Yes, case-law has established that a director may not be an employee where his or her powers as a director are so broad that his or her acts are essentially those of the company. This means that where a company has a sole director, rather than a board of directors, the sole director cannot also be an employee. Conversely, directors to whom specific powers are not delegated, but who are subject only to the general responsibilities of directors, may be employees. The distinction between directors and employees becomes difficult to draw in the case of a managing director, chairperson of the board, or other director to whom powers of management are delegated. The generally accepted view is that where only authority to carry out ordinary acts of management is delegated, an employment relationship may also exist, while powers of extraordinary management are incompatible with such a relationship.

What are the consequences of a director also being an employee?

Where a director is also an employee, the relationship between his or her two roles may take either of the following forms:

- it may be agreed in the service contract that one of the employee's duties is to hold office as a director; or
- his or her position as director may be quite distinct and independent of his or her role as an employee.

The form of this relationship could have an effect on tax and social security contributions, as explained below on page 131.

Is it better to avoid an employee relationship?

Yes, for both the company and the director it is often financially advantageous to try to avoid an employment relationship. From the company's point of view, the cost of having employees is much greater than that of retaining independent consultants. This is due both to the employer's high social security contributions, and to the fact that each year an employer has to set aside in a special reserve fund a proportion of the employee's salary as a provision for his or her entitlement to statutory severance pay when his or her employment ceases. The director him or herself may have greater opportunities for tax and social security avoidance if he or she is not an employee: for example, tax is deducted from his income at source only to a limited extent in these circumstances. However, it would be open to the authorities to challenge an obvious sham where, for example, a director was receiving substantial fees and effectively performing the role of an employee, but it was argued that he or she was not in fact such.

How is a director rewarded?

Again it is necessary to distinguish between the individual's capacity as director, and, where applicable, as employee.

In the absence of provision in the constitutional documents, the remuneration of the directors, *qua* directors, is fixed by the general meeting. The board of directors itself, however, with the advice of the college of statutory auditors, decides on the remuneration to be paid to individual directors who hold particular offices under the company's constitution. Under the Civil Code the remuneration may take the form of either or both of a fixed fee and a profit share.

The remuneration of an employee, however, is obviously a contractually agreed matter between the company and the individual.

Are there any restrictions on benefits which a director can receive from the company?

Yes, the Civil Code contains two important restrictions.

- *Loans* There is an absolute prohibition on directors receiving loans in any form, whether directly or through a third party, from the company or any subsidiary or holding company. Similarly, a director must not benefit from guarantees issued by any such company in respect of his or her debts. Breach of these prohibitions is a criminal offence punishable by imprisonment of between one and three years and a fine of between 400,000 and 4,000,000 L.
- *Acquisition of property by the company* During the first two years of a company's existence, the acquisition of property from a director for a price equal to at least one-tenth of the corporate capital requires the approval of the general meeting, on the basis of a valuation carried out by an expert appointed by the court. However, such approval and the valuation are not required in the case of transactions entered into under normal conditions in the course of the company's ongoing operations.

What are the tax and social security contributions to be paid by a director?

Again, the distinction between a director who is also an employee and one who is not is important. Three cases should be considered.

1 The employee who, as one of his or her duties as employee, holds office as a director. All his or her remuneration is considered as deriving from his or her employment. Consequently, he or she will be liable to pay income tax (IRPEF), levied at graduated rates ranging from 10 per cent to 50 per cent and deducted at source by the employer, who accounts for the amount deducted to the tax authorities. Social security contributions (to cover state pension and sickness benefit schemes) are payable for him or her as an employee. Contributions are payable both by the company and by the director, the amount being deducted from his or her salary by the employer who then pays the relevant authorities. The level of contributions depends on the sector in which the company in question operates (industrial, commercial etc) and on whether the director is employed as a manager (as is almost always the case, of course) or as an ordinary employee.

2 The director who is not an employee and who receives only fees in his or her capacity as a director is treated as a self-employed person, as a type of independent consultant supplying services to the company. The company makes a tax deduction of 19 per cent from the fees paid to him or her, payable to the tax authorities, but is not required to make any social security contributions, either by way of deduction from the fees

on behalf of the director, or on its own account. The director is responsible for making his or her social security contributions directly.

3 The employee who is also a director, but is not required to be such as part of his or her duties as an employee. In this mixed case, the rules outlined in paragraph 1 above apply to his salary as an employee, and those outlined in paragraph 2 to director's fees.

The above applies to directors who are resident in Italy. The position of non-resident directors is regulated by the relevant double tax treaties, but if no treaty is in force a withholding tax of 20 per cent is payable.

What is the basis of a director's authority?
The authority of a director derives from:

- the provisions of the Civil Code;
- the deed of incorporation and by-laws of the company;
- special powers delegated to individual directors (such as a managing director) by the general meeting or board of directors.

What are the powers of a director?
The Civil Code confers certain specific powers on the directors, such as the power to call shareholder meetings, to review valuations of contributions in kind, to challenge resolutions not adopted in conformity with the articles of association, to draw up the balance sheet and profit and loss statement and prepare the directors' report, to register statements of capital increase, to preserve company assets, particularly where the company is to be liquidated. However, subject to this, the Civil Code does not generally list in detail the powers of the directors, but simply states that they are responsible for the 'management' of the company. In practice the by-laws usually indicate more precisely the distinction between the respective roles of the directors and the general meeting.

For example, it is common to confer on the board or the sole director, as the case may be, full powers of ordinary and extraordinary management in relation to all matters not compulsorily reserved either by law (such as the approval of accounts, and appointment of directors and statutory auditors), or by the by-laws themselves to the jurisdiction of the general meeting.

Can the powers of the board of directors be delegated?
The powers of the board of directors can usually be delegated either to an executive committee (the delegation can be revoked at any time by the

board) or to one or more managing directors, provided this is permitted by the company's constitution or by the general meeting, but certain obligations, such as the preparation of the annual balance sheet, may not be delegated in this way and are the collective responsibility of the board.

Delegation of powers to one or more of the directors is usually coupled with the power to represent and bind the company in its relations with third parties (known as the 'legal representation' of the company). Under the Civil Code the constitutional documents must specify which directors have this status.

How are the powers of a director restricted?
The principal restrictions on the powers of the directors are:

- directors must respect the areas of authority reserved to the general meeting by the Civil Code and the company's constitution;
- directors must act within the corporate objects of the company;
- where there is more than one director, the power of management belongs to the board as a whole, subject to the possibility of delegation referred to above;
- a director who has a conflict of interest in relation to a particular matter must disclose it to the other directors and to the college of statutory auditors, and he or she must abstain from voting on the issue in question.

How are decisions made?
The Civil Code and the constitutional documents prescribe various decision-making procedures. Thus, the minimum quorum for a resolution is half of the directors in office, unless a greater number is fixed by the constitutional documents. Resolutions are passed by absolute majority (unless otherwise provided in the company's constitution), and a director's vote must be given in person, and not by a representative.

What about the rights of third parties?
There are various provisions protecting third parties acting in good faith in reliance on the authority of the directors, as follows:

- Where the directors entitled legally to represent the company carry out any acts legally and properly within the company's objects and constitution.
- Limitations on the power of such directors contained in the constitutional documents do not affect the rights of third parties, unless those third parties have intentionally acted to the prejudice of the company.

- The appointment of all directors must be notified to the Business Registry with the local court. Those who have the right of legal representation must deposit their signatures, and a note is to be made of whether their powers are to be exercised jointly or separately. These registrations are published in the official *Companies Bulletin*, and once this formality has been accomplished, third parties can rely on the propriety of the appointments, unless the company proves that they knew of grounds for invalidity.
- Acts performed by the directors which are *ultra vires* the corporate objects still bind the company *vis-à-vis* third parties acting in good faith.
- Where a director has failed to disclose a conflict of interest and has voted on a related resolution, rights acquired in good faith by third parties in pursuance of the resolution are protected.

What are the duties of a director?
The duties of the directors are both specific and general.

What are the specific obligations?
- There are various precise administrative obligations, eg:

    — to register their appointment in the Business Register;
    — to maintain the company books and accounts; and
    — to call general meetings of the company in certain cases.

- They may not carry on either directly or through an unlimited company any business competing with that of the company, either on their own account or for a third party, unless the consent of the general meeting is obtained.
- They must notify any conflict of interest to the other directors and to the college of statutory auditors.
- They must abstain from voting in a conflict of interest situation.

What are the general obligations?
- Directors have a general duty to manage the business of the company, and personally oversee its running.
- They must be diligent in their duties. The level of diligence required is that of the so-called 'mandatario', a standard which does not have any precise definition. It is an objective standard, ie that expected of a conscientious person accepting a directorship, and does not vary according to the personal capacities of the director in question. Thus, while a degree of diligence beyond that of the average person is required,

the director is not required to be an expert in all the fields relevant to the running of a business.

Whether that standard has been met in any particular case depends on the judge's evaluation of all the relevant circumstances, such as the type of company involved, its size and field of activity, the importance and nature of the transaction in relation to which a particular decision was made, the time available to make the decision etc.

Is the duty to oversee the running of the company personal or collective?

Each director's duty to oversee the running of the company is personal, which means he or she cannot remain a merely passive observer. Thus, a director may be in breach of duty even if he or she has not committed any positive wrongdoing him or herself if, with proper diligence, the director should have known what was happening and prevented it.

Similarly, a director cannot ignore adverse circumstances of which he or she becomes aware. The director must instead do all in his or her power to prevent prejudicial acts from being implemented, or to eliminate or mitigate adverse consequences. However, in this situation the duty of a director not personally at fault is limited to requesting a meeting of the board of directors to take appropriate measures. If such measures are not resolved, he or she must, without delay, record his or her dissent in the minute book and immediately notify the chairman of the college of statutory auditors (if there is one).

What about insider dealing?

In 1991 a law was passed in Italy making insider trading an offence for the first time. Anyone who comes into possession of specific, confidential information about a company by reason of his or her position (such as a director, statutory auditor or manager) is prohibited from buying or selling shares, whether directly or through an intermediary. Penalties for breach range from a fine of anything between 10 and 300 million L, to up to a year's imprisonment. The new law will be policed by the CONSOB ('Commissione Nazionale per le Società e la Borsa' – the regulatory body for the financial markets).

What are the potential consequences of a breach of duty by a director?

Directors who are in breach of their duty may be exposed to civil liability to the company, to creditors, and to members of the company and other third parties.

What is the civil liability to the company?

- A director who breaches the obligation not to compete with the company may be dismissed from office, and will be liable in damages.
- Where he or she breaches duties concerning conflicts of interest the director in question will be liable to the company for any loss suffered by the company as a result of the transaction in question.
- For breach of more general duties, directors are jointly liable to the company for breaches of duty, so that all directors answer for the fault of one or more individuals. Whether the facts giving rise to the breach of duty are attributable to particular directors is only relevant to the question of whether the innocent directors may claim an indemnity from the wrongdoers in respect of the liability to the company.

Are there any exceptions to the joint liability rule?

Yes, there are two exceptions to the rule of joint responsibility:

- where powers have been properly delegated to an executive committee or to individual directors, the other directors will not be liable for the way the delegated powers are exercised, unless they are in breach of their general duty to oversee the running of the company, and to take steps to prevent prejudicial acts of which they become aware;
- as mentioned above, an innocent director who becomes aware of wrongdoing may relieve him or herself of responsibility by calling a meeting of the board, recording his or her disagreement if corrective steps are not taken, and notifying the chairperson of the college of statutory auditors.

What is the procedure for taking action against directors?

The normal procedure for taking action against directors for breach of duty is the so-called 'azione sociale di responsabilità' (responsibility action). Such an action, which must be commenced within five years of the action complained of, is initiated by a) a resolution of the general meeting of the company (which may also be passed while the company is in liquidation), or b) by a judicial administrator, where appointed by the court (see below). The directors themselves may not vote on the resolution.

Can such a resolution result in the dismissal of a director?

Yes. If the resolution is passed with at least a fifth of the corporate capital voting in favour, the directors automatically cease to hold office, and the general meeting must provide for their replacement. In other cases, a separate resolution to dismiss the directors is required. The company can at any time withdraw or settle the responsibility action by agreement in the general meeting, unless a fifth or more of the corporate capital votes against the resolution.

Are there any other statutory rights of action against directors?

Yes. Apart from the responsibility action, the Civil Code gives members representing at least a tenth of the corporate capital the right to apply directly to the court if they suspect that there have been grave irregularities in the performance of their duties by the directors and the statutory auditors. The court can order an inquiry into the management of the company, and take appropriate steps, including, in the most serious cases, the appointment of a judicial administrator to manage the company.

What about the directors' liability to creditors?

The creditors may themselves have a direct right of action against the directors, who are jointly and severally liable where the directors are in breach of their duties relating to the preservation of the corporate assets, and the assets are consequently insufficient to satisfy the company's debts.

These duties to preserve assets include rules concerning distributions to members, purchase of the company's own shares, and subscriptions in kind, as well as the more general obligation to oversee the running of the company's business. Although the creditors' action may, and frequently does, overlap with a responsibility action by the company, it can be promoted independently, for example where, with the consent of the members, the directors have made improper distributions. If there are bankruptcy or liquidation proceedings, the creditors' action is pursued against the directors by the trustee.

What about the liability of directors to members and other third parties?

The Civil Code specifically provides that directors may be liable in damages to individual members of the company or to third parties who directly suffer loss as a result of their misconduct or fraud. For example, there may be a direct right of action where third parties have been induced to invest in or make loans to the company as a result of a misleading picture of the company's affairs in the balance sheet, or of misrepresentations made by the directors.

What about criminal liability?

In addition to civil liability, directors may find themselves exposed to criminal penalties (fines and/or imprisonment) as a result of certain types of breach of duty. While it is impractical here to list all these provisions the following should be noted among the more important:

- failing to abstain from voting in a board meeting on a resolution in a conflict of interest situation;
- falsification of accounts and other corporate documents, and improper payment of dividends;
- misuse of corporate information;
- impeding the college of statutory auditors or members from exercising their rights of control over the company's management;
- receiving loans from, or benefiting from guarantees issued by, the company or any subsidiary or holding company;
- breach of registration and filing requirements;
- spreading false information or other fraudulent conduct liable to affect the value of the company's shares or stock;
- fraudulent exaggeration of the value of property acquired by the company from promoters, founders, members or directors during the first two years of the company's existence, where the price paid is equal to one-tenth or more of the corporate capital;
- where a subscription in kind is made to the company's capital, and the value of the property concerned is fraudulently exaggerated;
- breaches of the regulations concerning the purchase by a company of its own shares;
- the acquisition on behalf of the company of holdings in other businesses which involve a substantial departure from the objects of the company.

Does the figure of the 'shadow director' or *de facto* director exist in Italy?

To a very limited extent the Civil Code recognises a figure analogous to the so-called 'shadow director' in English law, that is a person who is not technically a director, but to whom certain of the duties of a director apply. The rules governing the responsibilities of directors are expressly extended to managers appointed by the general meeting or pursuant to the company's constitutional documents, but only in relation to the functions delegated to them. Thus, for example, the extension does not apply to managers appointed by the board of directors itself unless the appointment is contemplated by the by-laws.

Apart from this express provision of the Civil Code, case law and academic writers have gradually begun to recognise the concept of the *de facto* director, who in practice exercises the managerial functions of a director, and who is therefore treated as owing the same duties and as being subject to responsibility actions. So far, the courts have tended to require some evidence of the consent of the members to the situation, so that the concept is typically applied to the case where a director's appointment was formally invalid, or where his or her term of office has expired but he or she has continued to act as a director. Certain academic writers, however, argue that the duties of directors should be owed by anyone who in practice exercises their functions regardless of their qualification to do so, and it is possible that the law may continue to move in this direction.

What is product liability and who is liable for it?

The 1985 EC directive on product liability has now been implemented in Italian law, imposing strict liability on producers of defective goods which cause damage to person or property, subject to certain defences.

In addition, normal contractual claims are possible in appropriate circumstances, such as where guarantees have been given as to the condition of a product.

As far as the position of directors is concerned, they may be exposed to criminal liability, like any other person directly involved, if they are responsible for the company putting dangerous goods on the market. Civil liability could arise if the company itself, in a responsibility action, were to seek an indemnity from the directors in respect of a product liability claim against the company, on the basis of a breach of the directors' general duties.

What are the consequences of a company insolvency for directors?

The insolvency or threatened insolvency of a company can give rise to two types of legal proceedings which affect the position of the directors:

- bankruptcy proceedings proper, which ultimately lead to the winding-up of the company; and
- various less drastic procedures (known collectively as procedure concorsuali), where there remains a possibility of saving the company.

What is the effect of bankruptcy proceedings as such?

The appointment of a trustee in bankruptcy proceedings results in the automatic transfer of the management of the company from the directors to the trustee, under the direction of the court.

What is the effect of the procedure concorsuali?

In the case of the procedure concorsuali, ordinary management remains in the hands of the directors, but is subject to the control of an appointed judicial commissioner who him or herself acts under the direction of the court. Acts of extraordinary management must be authorised by the court.

What about the civil liability of directors in insolvency proceedings?

As far as the civil liability of the directors is concerned, their position remains generally unchanged, except that, in the case of bankruptcy proceedings, the right to promote responsibility actions on behalf of the company or creditors vests in the trustee, with the consent of the court, which must hear the opinion of the creditors' meeting. Furthermore, the five-year prescription period during which proceedings must be commenced runs from the date of the insolvency, rather than from the date when the acts complained of were committed.

What about criminal liability in respect of insolvency proceedings?

The law on insolvency imposes criminal liability on directors in an extremely broad range of circumstances relating to companies which are declared bankrupt or otherwise become the subject of insolvency proceedings. It is important to note that in many cases mere incompetence or imprudence, falling short of fraud, may be sufficient to give rise to criminal liability. Consequently, directors of companies in financial difficulties would be well advised to consult their professional consultants early, with a view to minimising the risk of criminal sanctions in the event of future insolvency proceedings.

What are the most important 'insolvency' offences?

The most important offences which may be committed by a director in connection with insolvency are as follows:

- concealment or destruction of property;
- recognising non-existent liabilities with the intention of damaging creditors;
- destruction or falsification of accounts for personal profit or with the intention of damaging creditors;
- the maintenance of accounts in such a way as to make it impossible to understand how the affairs of the company have been managed;
- the making of fraudulent preferences with the aim of favouring certain creditors to the prejudice of others;
- causing the bankruptcy of the company by fraud or as a result of fraudulent transactions;
- incurring personal and family expenditure which is excessive having regard to the director's financial position;

- applying a substantial portion of the company's assets in purely speculative or manifestly imprudent transactions;
- entering into seriously imprudent transactions in order to delay the insolvency;
- aggravating the company's financial position by failing to seek a bankruptcy order at the appropriate time, or through some other grave fault;
- failing to honour obligations undertaken in previous insolvency proceedings;
- failure to maintain the company's books properly or at all during the preceding three years;
- contributing to the company's financial plight by failure to observe the obligations imposed by law on the directors;
- disguising the company's financial position while drawing credit from third parties.

How does an individual cease to be a director?
- At the end of the term prescribed in the appointment, a director ceases to hold office once the board has been reconstituted by the appointment of replacements. In the case of an SpA the maximum period of office is three years. However, directors are eligible for re-election, unless the company's constitution provides otherwise.
- A director may resign by written notice to the board of directors and the chairman of the college of statutory auditors. The resignation takes effect immediately if more than half the fixed number of directors remain in office, but otherwise only when new directors have been appointed to bring the strength of the board up to more than half.
- The general meeting has the power to remove a director at any time, including one appointed by the constitutional documents. In the absence of just cause, however, the director may claim damages.
- Upon the director's death.
- If one of the grounds of ineligibility specified above arises, a director immediately ceases to hold office.
- The board automatically ceases to hold office if the general meeting of the company resolves to start a responsibility action with the favourable vote of at least one-fifth of the corporate capital.

LUXEMBOURG

Steven Georgala, John Bellew

What are the main types of company which exist in Luxembourg?
There are two main types of company in Luxembourg.

- The 'Société anonyme' (SA) which is a joint stock corporation. This is the legal entity principally used for doing business in Luxembourg. The shares of a stock corporation are negotiable and may be quoted on the Stock Exchange. This form of company is mainly used by foreign investors for the establishment of a subsidiary in Luxembourg.
- The 'Société à responsabilité limitée' (Sàrl), a limited liability company which is the form usually chosen by smaller and medium-sized businesses. The shares in an Sàrl are not freely transferable, a transfer of shares being subject to the approval of at least three quarters of the shareholders. The company must have at least two shareholders, as Luxembourg law does not provide for a limited liability company established by only one shareholder. A limited liability company may not carry out activities relating to insurance, capitalisation and savings operations. A proposal to implement the EC Directive on single member companies is expected early in 1992.

Which rules govern the two types of companies?
Both companies are governed by the Luxembourg law on commercial companies dated 10 August 1915. This law has been subject to several amendments. The provisions concerning an SA are mainly contained in Article 50–60 of the Act, and those concerning a limited liability company are contained in Articles 179–203 and subsequent sections.

Does Luxembourg company law vary much from the laws of other states?
The Luxembourg law governing the management of a public company, an SA, is in many ways similar to the management of a company under Belgian law. Therefore only a few comments are needed in order to understand the system of management in Luxembourg companies. The management of an SA will be considered first, followed by the management of a Sàrl.

MANAGEMENT OF AN SA

What are the requirements for the management structure of an SA?
A public company, an SA, is managed by the board of directors which is authorised to represent and carry out the objects of the company. The board may appoint a chief executive ('administrateur délégué') to undertake the day-to-day running of the business, but this is not compulsory and is subject to the approval of the shareholders in general meeting.

In addition to the board every SA must have at least one officer called a 'commissaire'. A commissaire is essentially a type of auditor whose principal obligations are in respect of the accounts of the company, and does not really participate in the actual management of the company. It should, however, be borne in mind that a commissaire need not have any qualifications nor need he or she be independent.

How many directors must an SA have?
The board of directors of an SA must consist of at least three members. The law does not impose an upper limit on the number of directors, which is usually determined by the articles of association.

Who may be a director?
Any person, whether an individual or a legal entity, whether a shareholder or not, may be a director of an SA. Directors need not be resident in Luxembourg.

Who is excluded from being a director?
Luxembourg commercial company law contains no specific prohibitions about who may or may not be a director.

Who appoints a director of an SA?
Directors are appointed by the shareholders in general meeting. If there is a vacancy, the directors may appoint a new director. This requires the approval of the majority of the shareholders at the subsequent general meeting.

How long may a director serve?
A director may not be appointed for more than six years, but he can be re-elected.

What is the relationship between a company and a director?
The relationship between the company and the directors is defined as a 'mandate' and the board of directors is described as an 'organ' of the

company; an individual director may also be an 'organ' of the company where specific powers have been delegated to him or her.

How is the director rewarded?
Directors are not generally employees of the company, even if they are executive directors, and so do not receive a salary; although they may receive attendance fees and a share in the profits. It is possible, although rare, for a director (whether executive or non-executive) to be an employee, and if this is the case a salary, fixed by the shareholders in general meeting, will be paid.

What special benefits may a director receive from a company?
A director may receive loans from the company, and special pension benefits, and may participate in share option schemes. All payments made to directors resulting from their appointment must be disclosed in the annual accounts and report.

What are the tax and social security contributions to be paid by a director?
Remuneration paid to directors is subject to a withholding tax in Luxembourg. The tax base is the gross amount of the remuneration without any deduction. The tax rate depends on whether or not the director is a resident of Luxembourg.

Residents
A person is considered to be a resident if he or she is domiciled (eg has accommodation available for his or her use on a long-term basis) in Luxembourg; alternatively the person may prove that he or she is habitually resident in Luxembourg (ie present otherwise than temporarily). A person will be considered to be resident for any year in which he spends more than 183 days in Luxembourg.

If the resident recipient bears the withholding tax him or herself, the resident's rate is 20 per cent. Only the net amount (ie 100 per cent less 20 per cent) is then subject to income tax.

If the company chooses to pay the directors' fees net of withholding tax the effective rate is 25 per cent of the amount paid to the directors.

Non-residents
The tax rate for non-resident recipients who bear the tax themselves is 28.4 per cent. The non-resident director is not liable for more tax if he receives less than 53,000 Luxfr. If he or she receives more than this

amount, then he or she will also be liable for income tax. In this case, 20 per cent of the withholding tax is deductible and the remaining 8.4 per cent may be credited against income tax.

If the company bears the withholding tax, the rate is fixed at 39.66 per cent of the net amount paid, and 11.73 per cent of the net remuneration may be credited against income tax.

What is the basis of the director's authority?

The director's authority is derived both from statutory sources and from the articles of association. The articles may give wide powers to the directors and, in particular, may confer any powers not provided for by statute.

What are the powers of a director?

The directors have the power to undertake all acts necessary for the management of the company. They represent the company *vis-à-vis* third persons and also deal with the day-to-day running of the company, unless a special delegated director is appointed. If such a director is appointed with the consent of the general meeting, then the directors must draw up an annual report stating the remuneration and other advantages granted to the delegated director.

How are the powers of a director restricted?

The powers of a director are mainly restricted by statute, in particular by the provisions governing the distribution of powers between the different organs of the company (see below). The articles of association may provide for further restrictions.

In addition, the director may be subject to the control of one or more supervisors.

What are the statutory restrictions?

The statutory restrictions relate mainly to the allocation of the powers between the board of directors and the general meeting. The general meeting has the power to carry out any matters, except the management of the company.

Furthermore, according to Article 60 of the 1915 Company Law the board of directors needs the authorisation of the general meeting before it may delegate the powers necessary for the day-to-day running of the company to an individual director. If, however, a non-director is appointed the general agent of the company, approval is not needed.

What restrictions may be provided by the articles of Association?

The articles of association may define the powers of a director in a wide sense. They may confer any powers on the directors which the law does not allocate to the general meeting.

What about the control of the management?

A Luxembourg SA is subject to some extent to the control of the commissaire, but this is limited and relates to the financial situation of the company. In practice this does not really operate as a material control on the activities of the board.

What about a conflict of interests?

Contracts in which board members have a special personal interest must be reported to the board and to the subsequent general meeting (Article 57 of the 1915 Company Law).

What are the duties of a director?

A director of a Luxembourg company must ensure the proper and diligent management of the company. The relationship between a company and its directors is traditionally analysed as a relationship of mandate, with the directors being required to exercise the standard of care of the 'bonus paterfamilias' (ie the standard of care which the ordinary or reasonable person would apply to his or her own affairs) in the execution of that mandate. A higher standard of care is required from a director who receives remuneration for his or her office than from one who is not remunerated. In practice, if a director has any doubt as to whether any action might be a breach of his or her obligations, he or she should require the board to call a general meeting of shareholders.

Directors are responsible for all errors of management, whether positive or negative, which are not consistent with this standard of care, even if the actions have been accomplished within the limits of their powers and do not breach the law or the articles of association.

In addition to the general rules of liability set out above, there are certain specific provisions in the Companies Law which place specific liability on the directors. For example, in the case of any increase of capital pursuant to the authorisation of the shareholders, the directors are jointly liable for any part of the capital which is not subscribed and for any shares subscribed for by the company itself.

What are the penalties for a breach of duty by an executive board director of an SA?

Civil Liability

The basic rules determining the civil liability of directors of an SA are contained in Articles 58 and 59 of the Companies Law

- Article 58 provides that directors have no personal liability in respect of the obligations of the company.
- Article 59 specifies that each director is personally liable to the company in accordance with the general law for the due execution of the mandate accorded to him or her, and for the faults committed in the course of his or her management functions. Only the company may bring a claim for such a default by a board member, any proceedings being taken by the shareholders in general meeting. A wrongdoing director is liable to make good all damages which can be shown to be the immediate and directly foreseeable consequence of a breach of his or her mandate.
- Article 59 also imposes liability on directors in respect of breaches of the articles of association and of the Companies Law, which liability is owed both to the company and to third parties. Shareholders may not bring an action in their capacity as shareholders, but can bring an action as a 'third party' if they suffer loss which is personal and distinct from that caused to the company. The directors of a company are jointly liable in respect of any action under this provision in Article 59.

Examples of actions which could bring the second part of Article 59 into play include failure to convene the annual general meeting of shareholders; failure to produce, or late production of, the annual financial statements; and transactions by the directors outside the objects of the company. A board member may only be released from liability for a breach of duty if three conditions are met, namely:

- the board member did not participate in the breach of duty;
- no fault of any kind is imputable to him or her; *and*
- he or she reports the fraud to the very next general meeting of shareholders after the breach came to his or her notice.

It should be noted, however, that proceedings brought by third parties are not affected by any discharge granted by the shareholders in general meeting, nor by any separate renunciation by the company of any action.

Criminal Liability

Section XI of the Companies Law specifies certain specific penalties for breaches of certain provisions of that statute. The penalties range from fines (2500 to 150,000 Luxfr) to the penalties available for fraud which vary but generally include a short term of imprisonment or a fine of up to 150,000 Luxfr. Criminal liability will be imposed for actions ranging from the failure to include the required particulars in deeds to a deliberate omission to publish the accounts.

Is the company liable for the default of its directors?
The company is liable to third parties for acts committed by the directors in relation to their functions.

What is the scope of product liability in Luxembourg and who is responsible for it?
This is dealt with by Memorial A25, ie the legislation implementing the EC product liability directive.

What are the consequences of company insolvency for a director of an SA?
In principle, the directors are completely protected by the principle of limited liability and the separate grant of legal personality of the company. However, the directors will be called upon to contribute to a deficit if, by virtue of their bad management, they have caused loss to the company or to third parties which is a direct result of their culpable actions. It is often difficult to prove such an allegation as, in contrast to some other legal systems, there is no reversal of the burden of proof. Article 100 of the Commercial Companies Law is of particular importance here in that where a company has lost half of its share capital, its directors are obliged to call a shareholder's meeting to resolve whether or not to wind up the company. If this provision is not complied with then the directors may be held liable for all or a proportion of any subsequent increase in the company's liabilities.

How does an individual cease to be a director?
The office of a director may terminate for the following reasons

- death;
- retirement;
- expiry of his or her term of office; or
- dismissal or resignation.

How can a director of an SA be dismissed?
Directors appointed by the general meeting may be removed at any general meeting. The director is not entitled to claim any indemnity as a result of dismissal.

May a director of an SA resign?
Yes. A director of an SA may resign.

MANAGEMENT OF A Sàrl

Who is responsible for managing an Sàrl?
The business of a Sàrl is run by one or more business-managers who have a 'mandate' for the management of the company. These business-managers may or may not receive a salary and need not be members.

Are the requirements for the management structure of a Sàrl the same as for an SA?
There is no obligation in law upon a Sàrl with less than 25 shareholders to appoint commissaires, although companies with more than 25 shareholders must appoint one or more commissaires comprising a supervisory board. This board is appointed by the constitutive instrument of the company and re-elected at the intervals specified by the articles. The members may or may not be members of the company and the rights and obligations of the individuals making up this board are the same as for the Commissaires of an SA.

Irrespective of the size of the Sàrl, the accounts must be approved by the members in general meeting or by written resolution.

Who can be a business manager?
As is the case in an SA, any individual person who is not legally incapacitated may be a business-manager of a Sàrl.

Who is excluded from being a business-manager?
Luxembourg company law does not specifically deal with who may be a business-manager of a Sàrl.

Who appoints the business-manager of a Sàrl?
The business-manager is appointed by the shareholders in general meeting or, when the company is first established, in the articles of incorporation.

How long can a Sàrl manager serve?
The law does not govern how long the Sàrl manager can serve, so his or her office can therefore be for a specified or an indefinite period.

What is the position of an Sàrl manager?
The basis of the business-manager's office is a 'mandate', which means that he or she is not an employee of the company. Instead, he or she is described as an 'organ' of the company.

How is the business-manager of a Sàrl rewarded?
Luxembourg law does not provide for the special remuneration of the Sàrl manager. The articles of association may, however, provide for remuneration.

What about special benefits (loans etc.) granted to the business manager?
This area is not regulated by law and provided the directors take the decision for a proper purpose there are no restrictions on granting loans to the business-manager. It should be noted that the powers granted to business-managers do not include the ability to grant themselves such benefits.

What are the tax and social security contributions to be paid by a Sàrl manager?
The tax and social security contributions to be paid by a Sàrl manager are the same as in the case of a director of an SA (see above).

From where does a business-manager of a Sàrl derive his or her powers?
The powers of a business-manager are usually determined by law and the articles of incorporation.

What are the powers of a business-manager of a Sàrl?
Each business-manager is entitled to act in the name of and on behalf of the company to achieve the objects of the company in all circumstances, except where the powers are reserved to the company in general meeting. If the management of a company is composed of several managers, the articles of association usually deal with the question of whether they must act jointly or alone; if there is a requirement to act jointly, then this binds third parties. If the articles do not contain any description of powers in the case of several business-managers, then each manager has the power to act on his or her own on behalf of the company.

How are the powers of a business-manager restricted?
These powers may, however, be restricted by the articles. It should be noted that this restriction does not affect any third parties, even if they have notice of it.

What about the control of the management?

In a company with less than 25 shareholders, control is effected by the shareholders, who have the power to examine the annual accounts, eg the balance sheet and the profit and loss account, as well as the inventory. They are not, however, entitled to examine other company documents, except where a special order has been made by the court.

In a company with more than 25 shareholders, one or more commissaires must be elected by the shareholders, and their role is as described above.

What are the rights of a Sàrl against its business manager?

The business-manager is liable to the company for mismanagement and for breach of provisions contained in statute or the articles of association.

What is the liability of a business-manager?

By Article 68 of the Companies Law, the liability of a business-manager is determined according to the same rules as those applicable to a director of an SA. Accordingly, most of what was said previously in relation to directors applies to business-managers. Even those provisions relating to criminal liability apply in respect of those elements of corporate life which are also the responsibility of the business manager.

What are the consequences of company insolvency for a business-manager?

A business-manager is in the same position as a director if the company becomes insolvent.

How does an individual cease to be a business-manager?

A business-manager's office may be terminated by:

- dismissal or resignation;
- expiry of the business-manager's term of office; or
- death.

By whom can a business-manager be dismissed?

A business-manager can be dismissed by the general meeting.

What is the procedure for the dismissal of a business-manager?

The business-manager may usually be dismissed for important reasons such as incapacity, or breaches of statute or the articles of association. The articles may, however, provide for dismissal at any time without any reason.

If the business-manager does not agree with his or her dismissal, the decision is subject to the approval of the court. However, the articles may provide that such approval is not necessary.

May the business-manager of a Sàrl resign?
The business-manager may resign at any time.

THE
NETHERLANDS

Trude Exterkate

What are the main types of company which exist in the Netherlands?
There are two types of company in the Netherlands:

- the 'Naamloze Vennootschap' (NV), a public limited company comparable to the English plc or the German 'Aktiengesellschaft'; and
- the 'Besloten Vennootschap met beperkte Aansprakelijkheid' (BV), a private limited company comparable to the English 'Limited' or the German 'GmbH'.

What are the main differences between a NV and a BV?
- A NV can have registered shares as well as bearer shares and may issue share certificates. A BV can only have registered shares and may not issue share certificates.
- The statutes of a BV must contain certain restrictions on the transferability of shares (either the requirement that any transfer be approved by some organ of the company or the obligation on the shareholder first to offer his shares to the other shareholders). The statutes of a NV may contain such restrictions, but only for registered shares.
- The minimum share capital (issued and paid up) for a NV is 100,000 Dfl, while for a BV it is 40,000 Dfl.
- The powers of the shareholders' general meeting to issue new shares can be more easily transferred to other organs of the company in the case of a BV than in the case of a NV.
- The pre-emptive right of existing shareholders which arises on the issue of new shares can be more easily restricted or excluded in a BV than in a NV.
- In the case of payment in kind for shares, the statutory requirements as to the description and audit of the assets are stricter for a NV than for a BV.
- The restrictions on the acquisition and holding of the company's own shares are much more stringent for the NV (up to 10 per cent of the issued share capital) than for the BV (up to 50 per cent).
- A NV is not allowed to provide security to third parties wishing to

acquire its shares, nor to grant loans for that purpose. However, a BV may, under certain strict conditions, grant loans for that purpose.

- A NV is subject to more stringent requirements as to the distribution of an interim dividend than is a BV.
- The Dutch law on annual accounts provides for an exemption from the obligation to have accounts audited and to publish them for Dutch companies which form part of a group of companies and whose financial data is consolidated into the group accounts of another company within the EC, provided certain requirements are met (including a statement by the latter company that it will be jointly liable for any transactions entered into by the Dutch company). This exemption does not apply where the Dutch company is a NV.

There are no other differences of any substance between a NV and a BV. Holding and financing companies are almost always formed as a BV rather than a NV.

Which is the most usual form of company?

The BV is the most usual form of company in the Netherlands and is almost always used by wholly owned subsidiaries or by companies with a limited number of shareholders.

Does Dutch company law distinguish companies in any other way?

Yes. In Dutch company law a distinction is made between 1) large companies (which are dealt with below), whether NV or BV, and 2) other types of companies.

What is a large company?

A company is deemed to be a large company if a company has:

- an issued share capital and consolidated reserves of at least 22.5 million Dfl;
- a statutory employee representation through a workers council is required by the Works Councils Act, which applies to enterprises employing 35 or more employees; and
- 100 or more employees.

Are subsidiaries taken into account?

Yes. In establishing whether or not a company is 'large', other forms of business which act as its subsidiaries are taken into account. These subsidiary businesses may be other companies, co-operatives or partnerships.

What is the consequence of being a large company?

A large company must file a statement to this effect with the Trade Register, unless the company is subject to one of the following exemptions:

- if at least 50 per cent of the company's shares are held by a corporation which is already registered as a large company; or
- if the company is a holding company whose activities are solely restricted to managing and financing the activities of a group of companies, the majority of employees of which (ie of all the group companies) are employed outside the Netherlands; or
- if the company's activities are almost solely restricted to rendering services to the type of company referred to in the first example above.

Three years after a company has filed a statement with the Trade Register the rules for large companies will apply.

What happens when a large company reverts to being a small company?

The Office of the Commercial Register must be notified in order for the company's entry as a large company to be cancelled. The special rules relating to large companies will cease to apply three years from the date of this cancellation provided the company has not requalified as a large company in the interim.

What about Dutch company law?

For the moment, this is contained in Book 2 of the Dutch Civil Code ('Het Burgerlijk Wetboek') as amended new provisions taking effect on 1 January 1992. These provisions deal in particular with the liability of directors.

Are the requirements for the management structure of all companies the same?

No, although NVs and BVs are managed in the same way and are therefore dealt with together in this chapter. It is necessary to make a distinction between the management of a large company and other companies, because a large company must have a two-tier board, as follows.

- The first is the supervisory board, which controls the activities of the board of directors. Its powers are very wide and therefore its members are usually compared with the 'administrateur' of a French company.
- The second is the board of directors (the 'bestuur'), which must have at

least one member (a 'bestuurder') who undertakes the responsibility of managing and representing the company.

Are 'normal' companies, ie those which are not large, required to have supervisory boards?

A two-tier board is not compulsory for other companies, although it is quite usual.

How many directors must a company have on its supervisory board?

A large company, whether a NV or a BV, must have a supervisory board of at least three members, although in practice it generally has more.

If the company's articles of association do not provide for a certain number of directors, the company in general meeting may determine the exact number, unless the articles require the number of directors to be fixed by another part of the company, for example the supervisory board or the priority shareholders.

How are the members of a supervisory board in large companies appointed?

The members of the supervisory board of large companies are co-opted (for a term of not more than four years) by the supervisory board itself. Although the general meeting, the works council and the managing board are notified that there is a vacancy and are able to make recommendations in relation to it, it is the supervisory board who actually appoints. The general meeting or the workers council may object to an intended appointment, the main ground being that, upon such appointment, the supervisory board would cease to be suitably composed or the person proposed is incapable of performing his duties properly. Only in rare cases has an appeal proved to be successful.

How are the members of the supervisory board in other companies appointed?

The members of the supervisory board of companies not classified as large are appointed by the company in general meeting. There may, however, be provisions in the articles giving the holders of priority shares or the supervisory board itself the power to make binding proposals. This enables the holders of such rights to suggest at least two names for the appointment, from which the company in general meeting must make its choice. There may be deviation from the proposal but only when two thirds of those present and voting at the general meeting, who represent 50 per cent of the company's issued share capital, agree.

Who can be a director of a supervisory board?

Dutch company law does not require any special qualifications for company directors The board of management may be individuals or companies, except where a large company is concerned, in which case they may only be individuals. They may be, but need not be, shareholders of the company. Members of the supervisory board must always be natural persons, and may not be employees of the company. In exceptional circumstances (confirmed in case-law), the appointment as director of a certain person may be annulled if that person lacks the abilities and character necessary for the office of director.

Do the articles of association contain regulations concerning the membership of a supervisory board?

The articles of association may contain further conditions regulating the membership of the supervisory board of directors (eg the requirement that the director is a Dutch national). Such provisions are subject to the control of the Ministry of Justice, and the Ministry will not accept requirements which are too rigorous. For example, the Ministry has rejected as invalid a provision that only shareholders could be appointed as directors.

Who is excluded from being a director?

The articles of association set out who is excluded from being a member of the board of directors. However, any limitations contained in the articles must not be too restrictive as the supervisory board must always be able to use its own discretion in deciding who may become a director. Any restrictions will be subject to the approval of the Ministry of Justice which always has to approve a company's articles. Apart from the provisions contained in the articles, Dutch law does not require a director to have any qualifications or attributes.

Who appoints the directors of a large NV/BV?

The members of the board of directors of a large NV/BV are appointed exclusively by the supervisory board. There is no limit to the length of time they can serve in this position, nor are there any age limits after which a director ceases to be eligible.

Who appoints the directors in all other companies?

In all other NVs and BVs, the first directors will be set out in the articles of association. From then on, the directors will be elected by the shareholders in general meeting, usually by a simple majority vote, although the articles of association may provide otherwise. The articles must not require a majority exceeding two-thirds.

What is the relationship between a company and a director?

Although a director is an employee of the company, his position as an employee does not make him subordinate to other officers of the company or to the shareholders. Special provisions dealing with this point exist in Dutch legislation.

How is a director rewarded?

Dutch law provides that the level of directors' remuneration will be settled by the shareholders in general meeting, unless the articles of association provide otherwise (Art 135 of the Civil Code). Usually the supervisory board is given the power to establish the pay and conditions of the directors. The extent of the 'package' (usually a fixed salary and profit-sharing bonus) awarded to each director is included in the service agreement, but may also be set out in the articles of association.

Are there any restrictions on the benefits which a director may receive from a company?

Nothing prohibits a company from making loans to or providing guarantees which benefit its directors. However, if a possible conflict of interest arises, the company should be represented in any negotiations by members of the supervisory board.

What are the tax contributions to be paid by a director?

Any payments made to a director for services connected with the management of the company are taxable as income from employment—including other benefits such as interest-free, or interest-reduced loans.

Salary and disbursement payments made to resident directors, as well as the salaries paid to non-resident directors, are subject to Dutch personal income tax (unless agreed otherwise by tax treaty). A non-resident director will normally be required by the relevant tax treaty to pay income tax to the country in which he is resident.

Must a director pay social security contributions?

Yes, every person resident in the Netherlands pays social security. An additional contribution is deducted from each employee's salary and, as a director is regarded as an 'employee', he has to contribute to both systems.

What is the basis of a director's authority?
The legal basis for his authority is set out in the Dutch Civil Code, Arts 129 and 130, but details may also be set out in the articles of association and other contractual agreements made by the company.

What are the main powers of a director?
The directors of a NV and a BV have two main powers:

- the power to manage the company (Art 129);
- the power to represent the company (Art 130)

Is the power to manage the company exclusive?
Yes, the directors have unlimited power to run the affairs of the company and are totally responsible for their actions.

Is the power to represent the company restricted?
No, the directors have an unrestricted power to represent the company to third parties.

Is the power to represent a company individual or collective?
Each member of the board is entitled to represent the company individually, unless the articles of association provide otherwise. For example, they may provide that the company can only be represented by two (or more) directors acting together.

How are the powers of the directors restricted?
Under Dutch law, there are three types of restriction on the powers of a director:

- statutory restrictions;
- contractual restrictions; and
- the powers of another organ of the company.

What are the statutory restrictions placed on a director?
The statutory restrictions placed on a director mainly consist of the requirement in many instances that he should obtain the approval of another organ of the company before embarking on a course of action.

Statutory restrictions are also imposed on directors because of the powers vested in other bodies of the company, such as the shareholders in general meeting or, in the case of a large company, in the supervisory board which has the power to appoint or dismiss directors.

What about the participation of employees in the decision-making in general?

Under the provisions of the Works Councils Act 1971, the enterprises in which at least 35 persons are employed during more than one-third of a normal working week must establish a works council, which has the right to receive information concerning the activities and financial condition of the enterprise. It also has the right to advise the management on matters involving important company activities, such as mergers, recruitment and co-operation with other enterprises.

The approval of the works council is necessary for decisions regarding working hours, safety and health, pensions, profit-sharing, personnel policy etc.

What are the powers of a supervisory board?

They must approve various actions by the directors.

Which matters need the approval of a supervisory board?

If a company has a supervisory board, the articles normally contain a list of matters upon which the management may not decide without the prior approval of the supervisory board. If such a resolution is adopted without the necessary approval being obtained, it is nevertheless valid, although the non-observance of the articles will have internal consequences.

In addition, in a large company, legislation sets out a list of the minimum matters which need the approval of the supervisory board. These are contained in s 164 of the Dutch Civil Code and may be grouped into five different categories:

- matters dealing with the financial structure of the company such as

  — the issue, acquisition and/or cancellation of shares or debentures of the company,
  — the issue of debentures in a general partnership or limited partnership in which the company is a non-limited partner, or
  — the decision to be quoted or withdrawn from quotation on the Stock Exchange;

- a decision by the company to

  — enter into or terminate an agreement for any form of permanent co-operation with another company or legal entity,
  — become an unlimited partner in a general or limited partnership, or
  — participate in another company by acquiring a shareholding which

exceeds 25 per cent of the outstanding corporate stock of the company being invested in;

- any decisions concerning an investment by the company which represents capital expenditure of 25 per cent or more of the capital and reserves of the company;
- any decision by the board of directors to

  — modify the way in which the company amends its by-laws,
  — adopt any proposals to dissolve the management,
  — file a bankruptcy petition, or
  — temporarily suspend payments;

- any decisions concerning the employees, for example

  — the dismissal of a significant number of employees at the same time, or
  — a major change in the working conditions.

What are the contractual restrictions on a director's powers?
Any contractual restrictions on a director's power will be contained in the articles of association. The articles may restrict a director's power to manage the company by requiring the approval of the supervisory board, or another board, for matters additional to those set out above.

However, a director's power to represent the company cannot be restricted so as to affect third parties.

Is a board of directors controlled by another board?
In large companies, it is compulsory for the board of directors to be under the ultimate control of a supervisory board. A similar provision may be included in the articles of any other company.

The extent of the control depends on the size of the company. The task of the supervisory board is to supervise the management and to assist it by the giving of advice. The supervisory board has regular meetings with the management–in practice this happens, between four and ten times a year.

How many members must the supervisory board have?
When a company has a supervisory board, the articles will determine how many members the board may have. There is neither a maximum nor a set minimum figure. A large company, however, must have a supervisory board of at least three members.

The members of the supervisory board must be individuals, not corporate persons and must be no older than 72, although this is often reduced to the age of 70 in the articles.

Who is excluded from being a member of a supervisory board?

The following persons are excluded from being a member of a supervisory board:

- employees of the company;
- other people who render services to the company;
- employees of another company in which the company holds at least 50 per cent of the capital;
- members of the board of directors;
- members of a trade union who are consulted on matters such as work conditions; and
- legal entities.

How are the members of a supervisory board selected?

As a general rule, they are appointed by the general meeting although, exceptionally, a minority may be appointed by others. They are not representatives of the shareholders. The subject of their supervision is the business of the company as a whole. They must therefore also take into account the interests of the employees.

What are the fiduciary duties of the members of the supervisory board?

The members of the supervisory board are responsible for the proper performance of the functions entrusted to them and are jointly and severally liable for board decisions. An individual may, however, escape such liability if he is able to show that he took no part in the decision, or took proper steps to disassociate himself from the decision.

A member must act at his own discretion and independently. He cannot be the agent of any shareholders or those appointing him.

The acts of the supervisory board must be in the interests of the company.

Finally, members must conduct themselves in accordance with unwritten standards of reasonableness and fairness.

What is the main task of a supervisory board?

The main task of a supervisory board is to control the board of directors, which it may at any time ask for information regarding its actions. The supervisory board represents the company only when it has a conflicting interest with the board of directors, for example on any agreement between a managing director and the company.

What are the other powers of the supervisory board?
In large companies:

- the supervisory board must by law approve certain decisions of the board of directors (see also the paragraph on statutory restrictions); and
- the supervisory board appoints and dismisses the members of the board of directors.

Does a director have any statutory duties?
Yes, the board of directors is responsible for making sure that the financial statements of the company are prepared within five months of the end of the financial year and are published by depositing them with the Chamber of Commerce within eight days of the approval of the company in general meeting.

What are the duties of a director?
The directors of a company have the duty:

- to act in a responsible manner when handling the company's affairs (s 8 of the Dutch Civil Code); and
- of loyalty and good faith to the shareholders (s 7 of the Dutch Civil Code).

Does a main board director incur criminal liability for breach of his duties?
Yes, he may incur criminal liability, involving a public prosecution, for any act which he committed with intent to damage the company.

A director will also be criminally liable if he knowingly publishes incorrect annual accounts.

How can a main board director incur civil liability?
A director can incur civil liability in various ways:

- the general civil liability of directors under s 8 of the Dutch Civil Code attaches to all officers of the company;
- civil liability to third parties under Book I, s 1403(3) of the Dutch Civil Code;
- liability if the company becomes bankrupt;

- special tax liability according to Article 32(b) of the Wage Tax Act and Articles 41(a) and 41(b) of the Value Added Tax Act; and
- liability for incorrect accounts.

What is the liability arising out of s 8 of the Dutch Civil Code?

Section 8 to some extent defines the relationship between the director and the company. Thus, a director is responsible to the company for the proper performance of his duties. If he is ever in breach of this duty, the provisions of s 8 will apply. Whether or not the director acted in a reasonable manner is decided according to general principles of equity.

A presumption of negligence arises where there are:

- illegal transactions; or
- a failure to comply with the formalities of incorporation.

Are directors liable for loss arising from their negligence?

Yes, if the company suffers loss through the negligence of one or more directors, he or they are jointly and severally liable.

Is a director able to avoid this liability for negligence?

A director may be able to avoid liability if he can show that he was not a willing party to the negligent act, ie that he was overruled by the other members of the board or was actually unaware of the act. Thus, if the director can show that he did not approve of the act, that he contested the decision of the other directors and did nothing to carry out the decision, then he can avoid liability. A director may also be released from liability if a resolution to this effect is passed by the shareholders in general meeting.

What about civil liability to third parties?

Both a director and other employees of the company are liable to third parties. This is set out in Book I, s 1403(3) of the Dutch Civil Code which specifies when an employee is strictly liable for his actions (ie liable even without proof of any fault on his part). When strict liability arises, the employee will be primarily liable for the damage caused and the company itself will have secondary liability.

Does a director incur personal liability if the NV or BV goes bankrupt?

Yes. When an NV or BV goes bankrupt, the directors are liable for all debts which the company cannot meet out of its assets, provided it can be proved that the bankruptcy was caused by the negligence of the directors within the three preceding years.

Does negligence have to be proved?
No, such negligence will be presumed if a director has failed to comply with any one of the following duties:

- retaining the books and records of the company for ten years;
- producing annual accounts within six months of the end of the financial year;
- filing the annual accounts, plus explanatory notes at the Trade Register, if and when required by law;
- furthermore, if a partnership in which the NV or BV is a partner fails to comply with the special accounting requirements according to Art 6 of the Commercial Law, then liability may arise.

What about the special tax liability provided for by Article 32(a) of the Wage Tax Act and Articles 41(a) and 41(b) of the Value Added Tax Act?
A director must immediately inform the tax collector if he realises that any tax due cannot be paid. When such a notification is made, the tax administration will examine whether or not the non-payment is due to negligence by the director during the preceding three financial years. If negligence is found, the director will be personally liable for the tax debts. Liability will also arise if the director fails to file a notification. Similar provisions exist for certain social security and pension contributions.

What are the consequences of company insolvency for the directors?
As directors must act in the interests of the company, they must advise the supervisory board and/or the shareholders of any difficulties faced by the company in trying to pay its debts.

Unless the articles provide otherwise, the directors are not allowed to file a petition for bankruptcy without an order from the shareholders in general meeting.

How does an individual cease to be a director?
An individual may cease to be a director for various reasons as follows:

- he may be dismissed;
- he may resign;
- his office may be suspended;
- a petition to the court for the termination of his office may be filed;

- his appointment may be annulled if he is found to lack the ability and character necessary for the office of a director.

How may a director be dismissed?

A director can be dismissed at any time (s 134) by whoever appointed him, ie the supervisory board or the company in general meeting, who will have the authority to dismiss him. The workers' council must be notified of the dismissal of a director.

The articles of association may require the dismissal to be authorised by a special majority vote. However, the majority required must not be set at more than two-thirds of the votes cast, which themselves must represent 50 per cent of the capital.

The opinion of the shareholders must be sought before a director is dismissed by a supervisory board.

What are the consequences of the dismissal for a director's service agreement?

If a dismissal conflicts with the terms of the director's service contract (eg if he has a fixed term contract) or is in breach of Dutch employment law, then the company may be liable for any damages suffered by the director, unless he was dismissed for misconduct or other urgent personal reasons.

May a director be suspended from office?

Yes, a director may be suspended from office (s 147). If this happens, the director's employment contract will remain effective, but the director will not be allowed to do anything. Such a suspension can only last for a reasonable time before the director must either be reinstated or dismissed.

May a director resign?

A director can resign at any time. Compensation may, however, be payable by the director to the company, depending on the circumstances.

What about the court's power to terminate a director's contract?

The supervisory board may file a petition with the court for the termination of the director's contract if he has failed to carry out his duties or for some other important reason.

PORTUGAL

Carlos Aquiar

The main company legislation in Portugal is the Código das Sociedades Comerciais 1986 (CSC).

What are the main types of company which exist in Portugal?
There are two main types of companies in Portugal, the 'Sociedade Anónima' and the 'Sociedade por Quotas':

- the 'Sociedade Anónima' (which can be recognised by the letters SA after the name of the company) is the structure used by large enterprises which require a large capital base;
- The 'Sociedade por Quotas' is the structure usually chosen by smaller businesses, and can be recognised by the word 'Limitada' after the name of the company.

MANAGEMENT OF AN SA

What are the requirements for the management structure of an SA?
An SA can be managed in one of two ways:

1 The SA can have a 'Conselho de Administraçào', equivalent to a 'board of directors', which is responsible for the management of the company and which is headed by a 'Presidente do Conselho de Administraçào', the equivalent of a chairperson.

2 Alternatively, the company may have a form of management which is split between two different boards, an executive board (the 'Direcçào') and a supervisory board (the 'Conselho Geral'). The executive board is the main managing board of the company and is controlled by a supervisory board, the 'Conselho Geral'. It would be wrong to describe the members of the supervisory board as real directors, as they are concerned with the control of the management of the company. Their liability is, however, according to Article 81 of CSC, similar to that of ordinary directors.

The method of managing an SA with the 'Conselho de Administraçào', as described in (1) above, is by far the most usual method of managing an SA; the second type is rather unusual.

In the following pages, the provisions governing an SA with a Conselho de Administraçào will be considered under (1), followed by the rules applicable to an SA with an executive and a supervisory board, which will be dealt with under (2).

How many directors must an SA have?
1 The number of directors of a Conselho de Administraçào (the 'administradores') is fixed by the articles of association. There are no minimum or maximum limits on the number of directors a company may have, but there must be an odd number. If the paid-up share capital is less than 20,000,000 Esc, the articles of association may provide for a sole director.

2 The executive board must have an odd number of directors, again fixed by the articles of association, but it cannot have more than five members. The supervisory board must have more members than the executive board, but not more than 15. The number of directors is fixed by the articles of association, and must be an odd number.

Who appoints a director?
1 If an SA is formed by a public offer of shares, the directors are elected at the initial shareholders' meeting (Article 281, CSC).

   If the SA does not make a public share offer, the directors may be appointed by the articles or elected by the shareholders at a general meeting.

   The chairman is elected by the other members of the 'Conselho de Administraçào', unless the articles of association provide for his or her election by the shareholders in general meeting.

2 The members of the executive board are appointed by the supervisory board or in the articles of association. The president of the executive board is appointed by the supervisory board.

   The members of the supervisory board may be appointed by the articles of association or elected by the shareholders in general meeting.

Is there any limitation on the number of directorships which an individual can hold in any number of companies?
No, there is no such limitation under Portuguese law.

Who can be a director?
1 By law, members of the board of directors need not be shareholders, but they must have full legal capacity. It is possible for a company to be a director of another company and should this occur, the director

company should appoint a person as its permanent representative. This representative may be a director or an employee of the director company or a third party. There is no requirement that a director be Portuguese, so a foreign national or a company incorporated abroad may be a director of a Portuguese company.

2 Members of the executive board do not have to be shareholders, but must be capable individuals. Again, there are no restrictions on the ground of nationality. Members of the supervisory board, who have to be shareholders, cannot at the same time be members of the executive board.

What is the relationship between a company and a director?

As a general rule, the directors of a company are not regarded as employees; they have a special role within the company defined by the law as a 'mandate'. If an employee becomes a director then, unless he or she has been employed for more than one year, his or her contract of employment will become invalid on his or her appointment as director. If he or she has been employed for more than one year, his or her contract will merely be suspended while he or she is a director.

How is a director rewarded?

The director's remuneration is fixed by the shareholders in general meeting, taking into account his or her functions and the economic situation of the company. The director may receive a fixed sum and/or an amount equivalent to a certain percentage of the company's profits. This percentage has to be authorised and fixed by the articles of association.

Are there any restrictions on benefits which a director can receive from a company?

Under Article 397 of CSC, there is a total prohibition against a company granting any loan, guarantees, collaterals or any other form of security to a director of the company. (This provision does not apply if the granting of such a benefit is within the company's objects, provided no special advantage is granted to the director).

What are the tax and social security contributions to be paid by a director?

The remuneration of a director of an SA is taxed in the same way as an employee's salary, the income tax rate being determined by reference to the amount of remuneration the director receives. The directors of an SA are obliged to contribute to the social security system.

What is the basis of a director's authority?

The authority of a director is derived from three areas:

- the law, ie the 1986 Code;
- the articles of association;
- the decisions of the shareholders, other agreements (eg shareholders' agreements) and any other special rules.

What are the powers of a director?

1 Article 405 of the 1986 Code gives the board of directors wide powers to manage the company and deal with the day-to-day business of the company. The directors also have the power to act in the name of the company. The Code sets out the various powers and duties of a director, which include the power:

- to call a general meeting of shareholders;
- to prepare the annual reports and accounts;
- to authorise the giving of a guarantee by the company to a third party;
- To increase the company's share capital, although this power is subject to some limitations;
- to transfer the company's registered office; and
- to purchase, sell and encumber any assets (movables or immovables) of the company.

2 The members of the executive board have identical powers to those of the board of directors, but they will be subject to the control of the supervisory board.

The executive board is required to do the following:

- submit reports to the supervisory board detailing the current situation of the company;
- prepare the annual accounts and annual report; and
- submit documents showing the current strategy of the company.

The main power of a supervisory board lies in the permanent control of the executive board. To this effect, the supervisory board receives reports from the executive board and can examine the books and records of the company at any stage.

How are the powers of a director restricted?

Directors' powers may be restricted by the articles of association or by shareholders' agreements. In addition, the board of directors must act within the objects of the company.

However, some powers are retained by the general meeting of shareholders, such as:

- modifying the articles of association;
- approving the annual accounts;
- appointing and removing directors; and
- appointing and removing auditors.

What are the duties of a director?

As a general rule, all members of the board of directors or members of the executive board must respect the provisions of either the law or the articles of association which govern their activity as directors. They have special duties which oblige them to act with diligence and in the interests of the company (Article 64, CSC), and to report their activity to the supervisory board. They are forbidden, unless authorised by the shareholders in general meeting, to engage in an activity which competes with the business of the company.

What are the penalties for a breach of duty by a main board director?

Directors may be subject to civil and criminal liability in respect of their actions.

Civil liability

The civil liability of directors is contained in Article 72 onwards of the CSC and arises from the directors' failure to respect the articles of association or the law. Civil liability may arise if a director is sued for damages by someone who has incurred losses as a result of any act or omission on the part of the director, unless he or she can prove it is not his or her fault.

If a shareholder or a third party has incurred any losses, then they can make a claim against the wrong-doing directors. If the company has incurred any losses, then either a legal representative of the company (ie someone authorised to represent the company) or one or more shareholders holding a minimum of 5 per cent of the share capital are entitled to sue the director on behalf of the company.

Criminal liability

The criminal liability of directors is set out in Articles 509 to 529 of the 1986 Code, which provide that certain acts (including the unauthorised distribution of dividends, the irregular calling of a shareholders' meeting, or the publication of false accounts and acts considered to be contrary to the interests of the company), are punishable by fines or imprisonment.

Is a director jointly and severally liable for the default of his or her fellow directors?

Directors who do not actively participate in any wrongdoing or who vote against it at the relevant meeting may not be held liable for the wrongdoing of a fellow director.

Is a company liable for the default of its director?

The company itself is liable under civil law for the acts and omissions of its legal representatives, according to the general principles of tort as set out in Articles 998 and 500 of the Portuguese Civil Code. The company has the right to be indemnified by the director.

However, the company, as a corporate person, does not have criminal liability.

What are the consequences of a company insolvency for directors?

A director of an insolvent company may be liable for violations of legal provisions or the articles of association which result in the company becoming insolvent, provided it can be proved he or she was at fault. Thus a director may be required to account for all or part of the company's losses.

How does an individual cease to be a director?

A director can be removed from his or her position for the following reasons:

- when his or her term of office as a director comes to an end;
- if he or she resigns;
- if he or she is removed from his or her position by the shareholders. Any director of an SA may be dismissed at any time, and without any reason being given, by a decision of the shareholders in general meeting.

The removal of members of the executive board may also be carried out by the supervisory board, but only for a substantive justifiable reason.

If applicable, do the above-mentioned rules apply as well to a shadow director?

There is no such concept as 'shadow directors' in Portuguese law.

MANAGEMENT OF A SOCIEDADE POR QUOTAS (SQ)

What are the requirements for the management structure of an SQ?
An SQ is managed by one or more 'gerentes', who are business-directors who run the business and whose powers are equivalent to those of a director of an SA.

Who can be a business-director of an SQ?
The business-director of an SQ need not be a shareholder, but he or she must be a capable individual. A corporate entity cannot be a business-director of an SQ.

Who appoints the business-manager of an SQ?
The business-manager of an SQ is appointed by the articles of association or is elected by the shareholders in general meeting.

How is the business-manager rewarded?
The business-manager of an SQ has the right to be rewarded, unless the articles of association provide otherwise. The amount of his remuneration is fixed by the shareholders, but it cannot be an amount equivalent to a certain percentage of the company's profits, unless the articles of association authorise it.

What are the tax and the social security contributions to be paid by a business-manager?
A business-manager's remuneration is taxed as salary. The business-manager of an SQ must make social security contributions.

What is the basis of the business-manager's authority?
As with the directors of an SA, the sources of a business-manager's authority are:

- the law (1986 Code);
- the articles of association;
- shareholders' decisions and agreements, and any other special rules.

What are the powers of a business-manager?
A business-manager has the power to do anything which is necessary or desirable for the furtherance of the company's objects, provided he or she respects the shareholders' decisions and the articles of association. The business-manager has wide powers to represent the company. If a company

has several business-managers, then they must act together unless the articles of association provide otherwise.

What are the duties of a business-manager?

As with the director of an SA, the business-manager of an SQ must act within the objects and in the interests of the company, and is forbidden, unless authorised by the shareholders, to engage in an activity which competes with the business of the company.

What are the penalties for a breach of duty by a business-manager of an SQ?

The business-manager may be subject to civil and criminal liability, similar to the responsibilities of the directors of an SA (see above).

Is an SQ liable for the default of its business-manager?

As in the case of an SA, the SQ is liable for the acts of its legal representative, the business-manager, according to the general principles of tort.

What are the consequences of an SQ insolvency for its business-manager?

The business-manager of an SQ is liable for the company's insolvency in the same way as directors of an SA.

How does a business-manager of an SQ cease to be a director?

According to Article 257 of the CSC, a business-manager of an SQ can be removed by a shareholders' resolution at any time. The articles of association may, however, attach some conditions to this decision of the shareholders, unless there is a substantive justifiable reason for the removal. If there is not a justifiable reason, the business-manager may claim damages.

The resignation of a business-manager must be notified to the company. If the business-manager does not resign for a justifiable reason, then the company may claim damages from him or her unless he or she gave the company reasonable notice of his or her intended resignation.

What is the scope of product liability in Portugal and who is responsible for it?

Product liability in Portugal is specifically regulated by Decree No 383/89 of 6 November 1989 which incorporates the provisions of Directive No 85/374 into Portuguese law. Under Articles 8 and 9 of this Decree, manufacturers may face civil liability in respect of defects in their products, even if it is not their fault.

Are there any provisions under Portuguese law regulating insider dealing?

The Portuguese Government has recently approved new legislation regulating insider dealing in Portugal. Decree No. 142–A/91 of 10 April 1991, which has revoked Articles 524 and 525 of CSC which previously governed this area, came into force on 10 July 1991. Articles 666–9 of this Decree, which incorporate Directive 89/592/EC into Portuguese law, provide that insider dealing is punishable by a fine or up to two years' imprisonment.

SPAIN

Rick Silberstein

What are the main types of company which exist in Spain?
There are two main types of company in Spain as follows:

- A public company limited by shares or by guarantee, which must always be identified by the words 'Sociedad Anonima' or the letters 'SA' after the name of the company. This type of company is required by law to have a minimum share capital of 10 million Pta, 25 per cent of which must be paid up on the formation of the company.
- A limited liability company, which must always be identified by the words 'Sociedad de Responsabilidad Limitada' or by the letters 'SL' after the name of the company. This type of company has no shareholders, only partners who are required to invest only 500,000 Pta in total. The entire amount must be paid upon formation. The liability of each partner is then limited to the amount of his or her investment in the company.

The most common form until now has been the 'Sociedad Anonima', but following recent legislation imposing minimum capital requirements on public companies the 'Sociedad de Responsabilidad Limitada' form is likely to gain in popularity. It will, of course, be smaller businesses which will be affected by the legislation and will therefore adopt the 'SL' form.

What about the Spanish company legislation?
Both the Sociedad Anonima and the Sociedad de Responsabilidad Limitada are governed by specific legislation. The Ley de Socièdades Anónimas of 25 July 1989 ('Companies Act 1989'), which partially amended and adapted Spanish commercial law to comply with the EC directives and was approved by Royal Legislative Decree 1564/1989, governs Sociedades Anónimas. The legal regime relating to Sociedades de Responsabilidad Limitada is set out in Ley 19/1989 of 25 July (which modifies the Ley of 17 July 1953).

MANAGEMENT OF AN SA

What are the requirements for the management structure of an SA?
An SA can be managed in one of two ways: first the SA may have a

'Consejo de Administración' or 'board of directors'. This is formed when more than two persons are entrusted with the management of the company. The articles of the company usually provide that the board of directors has full authority to represent the company. Furthermore, the company is bound by any act of the board which falls within the company's objects, even if the board does not have specific authority to act in that particular way. The principal officers of the board of directors are the chairperson and secretary.

The chairperson presides over the company in general meeting but does not have a casting vote (in both cases the articles may, however, make specific provision to the contrary). The chairperson's approval of certificates issued by the company secretary is required, but without delegation by the board he or she has no further special powers.

The secretary, although an officer of the board, need not be a director. His or her signature is required on the minutes of both the general meetings of the company and board meetings. One further duty, which is undertaken as a result of tradition rather than law is for the secretary to keep the company books. The powers of the secretary extend to he or she being authorised to issue certificates on behalf of the company relating to such things as the contents of the minutes of board or shareholders' meetings.

It is common for the board to delegate all its authority to a 'Consejero Delegado' or managing director. If this is the case, the managing director and the chairperson do not have to be the same person, the division of power between them being decided in accordance with the general law and the articles. It is also possible for the board to delegate its authority to an executive committee, although the board may not delegate its duty to render accounts and present the balance sheet to the annual shareholders' meeting. This committee need not have the managing director, chairperson or secretary on it but its decisions are subject to review by the board to the extent provided in the articles or the rules established by the board as being applicable to the executive committee.

Alternatively, the company may authorise a sole administrator to manage the company. (When this is done there are no directors of the company.) The appointment of such an administrator is by the company in general meeting and that is the only body to which he or she is answerable. The powers conferred on him or her depend solely on the articles of the company.

Which of the two methods is the most usual?

It is probably more common for a board of directors to manage an SA

How many directors does a company have?

A board of directors must have at least three members. The legislation governing SAs does not lay down the maximum number of directors an SA may have, but this must be stated in the articles of the company.

Who determines the number of members of the executive committee?

The number of members of the executive committee is fixed either by the company's articles or by the board of directors. All members of the executive committee must be directors.

Are there any requirements for employee representation on the board of directors?

There are no requirements for employee representation on the board of directors of an SA, although work centres, as opposed to companies, with 50 or more workers must have 'workers' committees'. 'Work Centre' is a term of Spanish employment law relating to a 'productive unit' registered with the labour authorities. A workers' committee is the representative body of employees, through which the employees participate in the business.

Who can be director of an SA?

The Spanish companies legislation does not require a director to be a shareholder, although the articles of the company may provide otherwise.

It is possible for a company, if that is its only function, to be the director of another company, although in such a case a person must be appointed to represent the director company (they need not be a director of the director company). Details of directors must be reported to the Companies Registry.

Who is excluded from being a director?

The following groups of people cannot be directors:

- legally incapacitated persons;
- bankrupts;
- minors;
- those who have been convicted of a criminal offence and as part of their sentence have been prohibited from occupying public office;
- those who have been convicted of a reckless breach of the employment legislation;
- those who, due to their position in the government administration, are not eligible to carry on business in commerce; and

- civil servants who occupy positions relating to areas in which a company operates cannot be directors of that company.

It should be noted that nothing prevents a foreign national from being a director of a public company.

Who appoints the directors?
Normally the shareholders in general meeting appoint the directors. This method is used even in relation to the very first directors of the company.

Is the board of directors entitled to appoint directors?
If a director resigns during his or her term of office or a vacancy arises on the board for any other reason, the board of directors may designate someone from among the shareholders to fill the vacancy until the next general meeting of shareholders, when a new director will be appointed.

What is the relationship between a company and the directors?
The directors of a company, if that is their only function, are not considered employees for the purposes of the Spanish employment legislation unless they carry out duties not inherent in the duties of a director in which case an employer/employee relationship will be implied by law. The position is exactly the same for a sole administrator.

Are there any restrictions on benefits which a director can receive from the company?
If the articles of the company provide that the directors' remuneration shall be paid by way of an interest in the profits of the company, then that amount may only be deducted from the liquid earnings of the company after both the reserves established by statute and the articles have been covered *and* a dividend of 4 per cent (or more if provided for in the articles) has been set aside for the shareholders.

What is the basis of a director's authority?
The authority of a director is derived from two sources:

- the articles; and
- resolutions of the board of directors.

What are the powers of a director?
The directors have the following powers.

- Article 128 of the Companies Act 1989 provides that the representation of a company in court or otherwise shall be carried out by the board of directors as a collective body in the form determined by the articles. The board may delegate its authority; if this has been done then whoever has that authority may represent the company.

- The directors have the authority to call both annual and extraordinary shareholders' meetings.
- Directors may object to any resolution passed by the shareholders.
- The directors collectively appoint the officers of the board unless the articles provide otherwise.
- The directors may object to any void or voidable resolution passed by the board or any other associated management body such as the executive committee within a period of 20 days of its adoption.

What are the powers of the executive committee?

As mentioned above, the board may delegate all its duties (except the rendering of accounts) to the executive committee, with the result that in practice the executive committee can run the business of the company.

How are the powers of a member of the board of directors restricted?

A director may only act within the limits of the authority conferred on him or her by the board of directors, the executive committee or any person who may authorise him to act on their behalf such as the managing director. If a director acts outside his or her authority then the board may ratify this. If, however, the act not only exceeds the director's authority but also goes beyond the objects of the company then the act may not be ratified. When a director performs an act which is not ratifiable then he or she is personally liable for any loss resulting from it.

What are the legal obligations of a director?

Article 127 of the Companies Act 1989 states that the directors shall perform their duties with the diligence of a responsible businessperson and a faithful agent. In addition, they shall keep secret all confidential information relating to the company's affairs, even after having ceased to hold office.

On the matter of liability, Article 133 states:

- the directors shall be liable to the company, to the shareholders and to the creditors of the company for any damage that they may cause by reason of any acts contrary to the law or to the statutes or by reason of any acts performed without the diligence with which they are required to perform their duties;

- all members of the board of directors that performed the act or adopted the resolution causing the damage shall be jointly and severally liable, unless they prove that, not having taken part in such performance or in the adoption of such resolution, they were unaware of its existence or, having been so aware, did everything reasonably possible to prevent the damage or, at least, expressly opposed the said performance or resolution;
- where the act or resolution concerned has been adopted, authorised or ratified by a general meeting of shareholders, that fact shall not under any circumstances bring about exemption from liability.

The provisions set out above are compulsory and responsibility cannot be reduced by resolutions of the shareholders in general meeting nor by any provision in the articles of the company.

What are the primary obligations of the directors?

As stated above, the overriding obligation on directors is that they must perform their duties and obligations in the manner of an 'orderly business person and loyal representative'. It should be noted that the concept of a 'loyal representative' does not have a fixed legal definition and therefore has to be interpreted by the court in the light of all the facts as acting in accordance with the principles of good faith.

What are the rules governing directors' liability?

To whom they are liable

The directors have to perform their duties with the diligence necessary for the satisfactory management of the business. Consequently, they may be liable in the following ways:

- to the company (represented by the board of directors) for anything done in the performance of their duties;
- any act or omission of the directors which, although not damaging to the company's interests, causes damage to the shareholders will result in the directors being found directly liable to the company;
- finally, they will be liable to third parties who are creditors of the company and who are damaged by actions of the company which cause a decrease in the possibility of the company satisfying the lawful debts of its creditors.

Events of liability

The directors are liable for any actions as well as omissions (for example, the failure to do those things a responsible businessperson would have done) which either infringe the companies' legislation or the articles or which are not performed with the standard of diligence required of directors.

Extent of their liabilities
The directors are liable for all damage sustained by the company, the shareholders and third parties caused by the directors' wrongful acts. According to Article 1101 of the Spanish Civil Code, the word 'damage' covers both actual damage and 'lucrum cessans' (future profits). If the board of directors has a legal adviser, his or her intervention will be taken into account for the purposes of evaluating and measuring the liability of the directors. Whether this intervention decreases or increases liability is something decided by the tribunal concerned on the facts of the particular case.

Nature of their liabilities
Article 133 of the Companies Act 1989 provides that all the members of the board that performed the act or adopted the resolution causing the damage shall be jointly and severally liable. Each director is responsible for every act taken by the board of directors, and action can be taken against them individually or as a group. In accordance with Article 1214 of the Spanish Civil Code, all members are presumed liable and it is for a director who wishes to escape responsibility to prove that he or she took no part in the act which caused the damage.

There are, however, three cases where the director will not be held liable.

- If he or she has not intervened in the adoption or execution of the resolution and, in addition, was unaware of the existence of the resolution in question.
- If, despite knowledge of the existence of the resolution, the director did all that was necessary to avoid the damage. It appears that, for this exception to apply, the director concerned must have challenged the resolution and that his or her opposition should be noted in the company's records.
- If the director manifestly opposes the resolution. Abstention is not sufficient, the director must actively demonstrate his or her opposition to what is proposed and demand that his or her views be registered in the minutes of the board of directors.

Statute of limitations
There is a four-year limitation period on a director's liability, commencing

on the date of his or her resignation or dismissal as director (Article 949 of the Commercial Code).

What is the criminal liability of directors?

The criminal liability of directors is governed by the general provisions of the penal code; there are no specific provisions relating to crimes by directors.

Criminal liability is strictly personal and non-transferable, ie only individuals can commit crimes, not entities or companies. As a result, a board of directors cannot commit a crime – only its members can. Individual directors may face criminal liability if they have personally carried out criminal acts while directors of the company, although they will only be held responsible for their own actions or omissions, not those of their fellow directors.

A director is also personally liable for any award of civil damages made as a result of any criminal act. If a director is totally or partially insolvent then, provided an attempt has been made to recover from him or her first and he or she is unable to satisfy it, the company is liable.

What are the tax liabilities of directors?

Directors will be liable for the taxes of the company, where the company is unable to satisfy them, in the following situations:

- if they fail to take the steps necessary for the fulfilment of a company's obligations regarding tax payments under Article 40.1 of the General Tax Law 1963;
- if they consent to the non-compliance with such obligations by their subordinates;
- if they adopt a resolution which makes infringement of the tax legislation possible.

A director is, of course, taxed on his or her income which includes remuneration from the company whether received pursuant to a service contract or not.

To what extent is a director liable for a product liability action against the company?

The Consumer Protection Law 1984, which was passed prior to the EC directive of 1985 concerning product liability, does not specifically address the issue of directors' liability. The consumer or user, as the case may be, has a right to be indemnified for damages derived from the consumption of defective goods, or the use of products or services which prove to be defective, unless the damages are caused entirely by the fault of that consumer or user. Under Spanish law the manufacturer, importer, vendor or supplier of the defective products may be liable for the damages suffered by consumers or users. If this means that it will be a company which is liable for a consumer or user's injury, and liability can be traced to a breach of duty on the part of a director, then the company itself, the shareholders or even third parties may initiate an action against the director concerned.

It should be noted that draft legislation to implement the 1985 EC directive is currently before the Spanish Parliament.

What are the consequences of a company insolvency for a director?

The directors must call a general meeting of shareholders to adopt a resolution to dissolve the company in the following situations:

- if the company is no longer carrying on business;
- if it is no longer possible to carry on the objects of the company;
- if the administrative bodies of the company are 'dead-locked' with the result that the company is unable to function;
- where, as a consequence of losses suffered by the company, the company's assets are reduced to less than half the share capital and the share capital is not increased or reduced sufficiently to bring the debt – equity ratio of the company in line with that required by the Companies Act 1989;
- when the share capital is reduced below the minimum legal requirement.

In addition to the circumstances listed above, the articles may require the directors to call a general meeting to adopt a dissolution resolution upon the occurrence of specific events. If the result of the shareholders' resolution is against dissolution or if it is not possible to obtain the necessary resolution, then the directors are obliged to apply for a judicial dissolution of the company. The directors are severally liable to the company, the shareholders and the creditors if they do not comply with the duty to call a general meeting within a period of two months from the occurrence of these events mentioned above.

The authority of the directors to conclude new contracts and to enter into new obligations ceases the moment the company is declared to be in liquidation, although the former directors must, if required, assist the liquidator in the performance of his or her functions.

How does an individual cease to be a director?

An individual will cease to be a director (and consequently the managing director, chairperson or sole administrator) if any of the following occurs.

- A director may be removed at any time by a resolution of the shareholders in general meeting;
- Upon the request of any shareholder, any director who has violated any of the prohibitions mentioned above must immediately be dismissed by a resolution of the board of directors. This will not affect any liability he or she may incur for breach of duty, in accordance with Article 133 of the Companies Act.
- Any director who is also a director of a competing company, or who in any way has interests which conflict with those of the company, may upon the request of any shareholder be dismissed by a resolution of the shareholders in general meeting.
- Finally, a director may resign of his or her own accord.

If removed as a director then an individual will also cease to be the managing director or chairperson of the company. The reverse, however, is not true and an individual may remain as a director if removed from the post of managing director or chairperson.

Following removal as a director there are certain circumstances in which the individual will be disqualified from acting as such in the future. A disqualification order may be made as part of his or her sentence where a director has been convicted of a criminal offence or where there have been serious breaches of the civil law or labour legislation.

MANAGEMENT OF AN SL

Are the requirements of the management structure of an SL the same as in the case of an SA?

The structure of an SL is not exactly the same as that of an SA. In principle the company is managed by its directors, but the will of the partners, expressed by a majority, governs company life. There may well be blurring of the distinction between 'partners' and 'directors' since a partner may be both. A director is appointed by a majority of the partners or by using a mechanism set out in the constitutional deed. When the number of partners exceeds 15, or when provided for in the constitutional deed, the majority must meet as a general meeting. The acts of the directors are regulated by the terms of the constitutional deed and by the will of the majority of the partners together with the general rules applicable to directors of an SA, as set out above, except where different rules are established by the law governing SLs.

It is interesting to note that while the law does not expressly permit an SL to have a chairperson, managing director or sole administrator, these positions exist in SLs. This fact is due to the general rule that where special provision is not made by the law in respect of SLs the law governing SAs will be applied.

Are there any limits on directors of an SL?
The directors of an SL may not, either for their own benefit or for that of another, engage in the same type of business as that of the SL.

For how long may a director remain in office?
A director of an SL may remain in office for the period indicated in the company's articles.

How are the directors of an SL dismissed?
The directors may be dismissed at any time by a resolution of the partners representing the majority of the share capital of the company, except when the director concerned has been appointed in the constitutional deed. In this latter case, a majority of the partners representing at least two-thirds of the company's increased share capital must vote in favour of his or her dismissal. The increased majority is required here because the dismissal effects a modification of the articles of the company.

The reasons for dismissal are the same as those for SAs.

UNITED KINGDOM

Kevin Tuffnell

What are the main types of company which exist in the UK?

- The private limited company.
- The public limited company (plc).

Are they governed by one particular Act?

No. The Companies Act 1985 consolidates many previous statutes and provides a body of law for the formation and running of different types of companies, but other Acts are also important, such as the Insolvency Act (1986). Sometimes different rules apply to private and public companies, but the relationship between ownership and management for public and private companies is the same. Before looking at the responsibilities and duties of directors it is important to understand the different company structures.

What is the most commonly used company structure?

The company limited by shares, ie where the contribution of members to company debts in the event of an insolvent winding-up is limited to the nominal amount of their shares (together with any premium they have paid, or agreed to pay), is the most commonly used company structure, although other forms of company are possible, eg:

1 the unlimited company (in which members are liable to contribute without limit to the debts of the company in the event of an insolvent winding-up);

2 the company limited by guarantee; and

3 the company incorporated by charter.

Two and three are unusual and used only in specific circumstances.

What is a private limited company?

This is a company in private ownership which is normally limited by shares. This is the most suitable structure for small businesses where control is centred in the hands of a few shareholders.

What is a public limited company?
This is a company limited by shares, and which is permitted to offer shares for sale to the public, although it is not uncommon for a public company to remain in private ownership. It is more appropriate for larger businesses which have a greater need for easy access to funding through a more diverse capital base.

Do the Companies Acts and general legal principles apply equally to private and public companies?
Yes, the main body of statutory rules and general legal principles apply to private and public companies to govern the way they are run, and the relationship between ownership and management.

What are the differences between public and private companies?
The Companies Act 1985 sets out several differences between public and private companies. The most important is that a private company may not, but a public company may, raise capital by an issue of its shares to the world at large. Public companies are consequently subject to additional administrative restrictions for which its directors are responsible.

Are shares of all public companies traded on a stock exchange?
No, but if in addition to the general company legislation the public company complies with the relevant rules, its shares may be traded freely on one of the markets of the Stock Exchange (the official list or the unlisted securities market).

How is the price of a public company's shares decided?
The market price of shares may fluctuate, effected by differing factors including the performance of the company, its sector, market performance or the state of the economy as a whole.

Are there any differences between the duties of directors of public and of private companies?
The duties of a director of a private or a public company are substantially the same. There is a duty to be competent, besides duties arising out of the relationship of trust which exists between a company and its directors. The public company director must bear in mind the additional statutory requirements which arise out of the status of the company (see below).

What are the requirements for the management structure of these companies?
The management structure imposed by the Companies Act applies

regardless of whether the company is public or private, limited or unlimited.

The business and day-to-day management is the responsibility of a board of directors appointed by the shareholders of the company. Thus, the company is owned by the shareholders and run by the directors.

Can shareholders be directors?

Yes, in smaller companies individuals will frequently be both directors and major shareholders, but the distinction is an important one because different rights, duties and powers will attach to each role. It is important for an individual to distinguish between his or her position as director, and as shareholder. The two should not be confused.

Do shareholders have the right to control the day-to-day running of a company?

The shareholders do not normally have a right by virtue of their position as shareholders to control or interfere with the day-to-day running of the business, but they retain the ultimate sanction of dismissal of a director they do not consider to be performing satisfactorily.

How is the board of directors made up?

The board of directors is composed of:

- executive directors (in effect professional employees with skills in the particular areas of a company's business);
- non-executive directors who, although officers of the company, are not its employees, and are not involved in the running of the company's business. They sit as directors to represent the shareholders' interests, and to regulate the management of the company by the executive directors.

What are the articles of association of a company?

The company's articles of association (usually referred to as 'the articles') is the document which regulates the company's internal affairs.

What should the articles of association contain?

The articles should contain details of the appointment and powers of the directors and secretary, the issue and transfer of shares, the conduct of meetings, and include other matters such as voting rights, how dividends should be paid, and details concerning accounts and audits. Model articles are contained in Table A in the Companies Act (Tables A to F) Regulations 1985.

What is the memorandum?
Every registered company must also have a Memorandum which regulates the company's external affairs.

What does the memorandum have to include?
The memorandum must include the name of the company, together with its registered office, its objects, the fact that the liability of members is limited (for a limited company) and the amount of its share capital.

In addition a public company must include a statement that it is a public company, and its name must end with the words 'public limited company' or 'plc'.

Do the directors have total control with regard to the running of a company?
No, certain decisions require shareholder approval of either a simple majority or 75 per cent of the votes cast. The directors will therefore on occasions have to call general meetings of the shareholders, and put their proposals before the shareholders for approval.

What about the annual general meeting?
Every company must hold an annual general meeting unless, in the case of a private company, its shareholders elect to dispense with such meetings. The annual general meeting provides a general opportunity for the shareholders to review the management of the company by the directors and state any grievances which they may have.

How many directors must a company have?
Under the Companies Act 1985, a private company need only have one director, unless the articles of association of the company require a greater number to be appointed. A public company must always have at least two directors, although once again the articles may require a greater number.

What is the norm?
It will often be convenient for a small, private company to have only one director, but between five and ten would be usual.

Who may appoint the directors?
The appointment of directors is governed by the company's articles of association. Thus:

- under Table A the position is that directors are appointed by a simple majority of the shareholders in general meeting;
- Table A provides that the board of directors is authorised to appoint persons to the board as additional directors, or to fill a vacancy which has arisen on the board;
- when a company is established as a joint venture between different parties, each party will frequently be given the right to nominate its own directors. Then it is usual for the constitution of the company to provide that no decisions can be taken at a board meeting unless a minimum of at least one director appointed by each side is present to provide a quorum.

Who can be a director?
Both individuals and other companies may be company directors, unless they are prohibited by law from holding office.

Who is excluded from being a director?
- It is a criminal offence for bankrupts to be company directors.
- The Companies Disqualification Act 1986 provides a procedure for preventing those who have proved themselves to be unsuitable to hold the office of director from continuing to do so.
- Insane persons.
- Minors.

If a company is a director of another company, it must in turn act through its properly appointed officers, usually members of its own board of directors.

Is there an age limit?
Unless the articles provide otherwise, a director of a public company, or of a subsidiary of a public company, must vacate his or her office at the annual general meeting following his or her 70th birthday, but may be reappointed by the shareholders.

What is the relationship between a company and a director?
A professional director involved in the management of a company has various elements in his or her relationship with the company, as follows.

- The director is the means by which the company acts, its representative to third parties and its agent in business; and his or her role is governed by the company's constitution.
- If the director is an executive director he or she will also be its

employee, entitled to a salary and other benefits along with all its other employees. Executive directors are usually given a service agreement clearly setting out their precise functions and rewards. Service agreements are most common in larger companies where executives are appointed with specific areas of expertise and responsibility, and where management and ownership of the company are often in different hands.

Is this distinction between service and other agreements important?

Yes, and the distinction becomes more apparent as the size of the company increases. Small companies often have few directors, performing general functions, and who are probably the owners of the business. By contrast, larger enterprises have a greater need for more specialised skills, and directors are appointed with precise areas of responsibility, such as finance or production. They have specific powers in their own area of expertise, and their service agreements will reflect their particular role.

What about conflicts of interest?

Sometimes the interests of the director are not in accord with those of the company, and a director must seek to ensure that his or her own interests, and duties owed to others, do not conflict with the duty to act in the best interests of the company.

Are there different types of directors?

Yes. Some titles reflect the division of professional duties (eg 'finance director' or 'marketing director'), or indicate the constitutional roles of the directors. The most important types are:

● managing director;
● chairperson;
● alternate directors;
● non-executive directors;
● shadow directors.

What is the role of the managing director (MD)?

Larger companies commonly appoint a managing director, who is delegated to run the business of the company, but is under the control of the board, to whom he or she must report.

The managing director may have wide-ranging powers, although it is for the board of the company to determine the extent of those powers.

The appointment of a managing director assists effective decision-making, and can be appropriate in small companies where the managing director will often be the driving force, but also in large companies, where ownership may be diverse and the business complex.

What is the role of the chairperson?

The chairperson of the board is usually appointed by the board, and his or her main function is procedural. The chairperson presides at meetings of the board of directors, and at shareholders' meetings. His or her job is to steer the business of the meeting so that effective decisions are taken in good order. The articles may give an extra deciding vote to the chairperson to avoid a deadlock in a 'tied' vote of the directors or shareholders.

The chairperson will often be a non-executive director, whose appointment is designed to safeguard the position of the shareholders, and to maintain a detached view in difficult circumstances.

What is the role of an alternate director?

Alternate directors are temporary delegates to exercise the votes of the directors in their absence. Generally a person may be appointed as an alternate director if he or she is:

- already a director; or
- a third person approved by the board.

What are the voting rights of alternate directors?

An alternate director is entitled to attend board meetings and vote in place of his or her appointor, as well as doing anything else the appointor may do in his or her capacity as a director. An alternate director is not considered to be the agent of his or her appointor, who is liable only for acts of the alternate which he or she expressly authorises.

Why appoint an alternate director?

In order to ensure that the views of a director unable to attend a board meeting in person are properly represented to the other directors.

What is the role of a non-executive director?

These are officers of the company who are not its full-time employees. Because of their position – independent of the day-to-day running of the company – and their lack of personal involvement as employees, non-executive directors can exercise a supervisory and controlling function, often on behalf of the shareholders. They also frequently take a leading role in the settlement of board disputes.

Under UK law there is no distinction between the executive and non-executive director. Both have the same powers and responsibilities.

It is generally accepted that the fees paid to non-executives directors should be relatively modest, because they normally devote only a small proportion of their time to the company's affairs, and because their independence would be jeopardised if they were to become largely or wholly dependent on their directors' fees.

What is the role of a shadow director?

Strictly, a shadow director is not a director at all, and is not appointed as an officer of the company by any formal procedure. None the less, the Companies Act 1985 recognises that companies are frequently influenced and controlled by non-directors, for example majority or substantial shareholders, who are in a position of commercial strength and thereby able to give instructions to the board of directors which will be followed. A good example of this is where groups of companies act in accordance with instructions coming from the parent company. In order to prevent avoidance of the restrictions and responsibilities imposed on directors, the statute classes individuals or companies exercising such influence as 'shadow directors', and extends certain of those restrictions and responsibilities to them.

When is a shadow director not a shadow director?

As it depends on influence rather than strict procedure, whether or not a person is a shadow director is often unclear. Directors should take legal advice if they are unsure whether a shadow directorship has arisen. However, it is clear that professional advisers acting as such will not be shadow directors.

How is a director rewarded?

- Directors are not strictly entitled to any payment for their services as officers of the company, unless this is authorised by the articles of association.
- Directors employed by the company are paid as employees. Their remuneration packages are commonly referred to as their 'emoluments', and must be disclosed in the company's accounts.

What are 'emoluments'?

The expression covers a much wider variety of benefits than merely fees or salary, and includes all benefits in kind. Sophisticated remuneration packages are often involved, in order to provide incentives for professional directors. These include cars provided for the director's private and personal use, private health cover, life assurance benefits, performance-related bonuses and contributory or non-contributory pension schemes. There has lately been a growth in the number and forms of directors' share and share option schemes, whereby directors are given a right to take shares in the company at a future date on a beneficial tax basis. Improved performance and profits increase the value of the shares and thus motivate the director to greater performance.

The bigger the company the more likely it is that there will be sophisticated remuneration packages, and closely defined duties and responsibilities, all contained within the directors' service agreements.

Are small company packages the same?

Sometimes, but complex packages tend to be inappropriate in a small company. The director's own finances are likely to be tied to the fortunes of the company, and increased profits will be reflected in a higher salary, or may instead be taken out in the form of share dividends if, as is often the case, the directors are also substantial shareholders. In some companies the form of the directors' reward will be influenced by accounting and tax considerations, rather than by rigid contractual entitlements.

What tax and social security contributions must be paid by a director?

Income tax

A person resident in the UK is taxable on his or her worldwide income. Non-residents are generally only taxable on income arising in the UK.

For UK tax purposes income is classified under six schedules. The most important is Schedule E, as it includes all income and emoluments widely defined, including benefits in kind, as well as fees or salary for any office (eg a directorship) or employment of an individual.

If a director is another company, payments made in respect of the directorship will be subject to corporation tax rather than income tax.

Social security

In addition to income tax, a person employed in the UK is liable for national insurance contributions at a current rate of up to 9 per cent of gross earnings up to a current maximum of £122.53 per month.

Further, the company itself must pay further national insurance contributions up to a maximum of 10.45 per cent of gross earnings to the Inland Revenue. Unlike personal contributions, however, there is no ceiling on the actual amount that an employer may be required to contribute.

A non-UK national employee who arrives in the UK to take up employment may sometimes obtain exemption from national insurance liability for a one-year period from his or her arrival in the UK.

Capital gains tax
A director may incur liability for capital gains tax upon a disposal (or in certain circumstances a deemed disposal) of an asset at a profit.

Conclusion
The tax position of directors is frequently complicated, and, as with any individual, liability can also be incurred under inheritance tax (which deals with gifts and death duty), and under direct taxes such as value added tax (VAT) and stamp duty. Directors, especially overseas nationals only temporarily resident in the UK, would be well advised to take specific professional advice on their tax position.

Are there any restrictions on the benefits which a director can receive from a company?

Yes. Smaller companies are often the means by which individuals carry on business, but a company is a separate person at law, and it is vital to separate the personal financial concerns of the director from those of the company he or she represents. Companies legislation therefore prohibits certain forms of benefit. The underlying principle is that because of his or her position, credit facilities from the company to the director and transactions in which a director contracts with the company are undesirable.

What are the restrictions on benefits?

Sections 311 to 344 of the Companies Act 1985 impose widely-drawn restrictions on benefits both on transactions with the director and persons connected with him or her, and on indirect transactions involving third parties. These provisions seek to ensure fair dealing by directors.

The most significant restrictions are as follows.

- It is prohibited for the company to pay a director any remuneration free of income tax (s 311 of the Companies Act).
- It is unlawful for a company to make a payment for compensation for loss of office as a director, unless this has been approved by the shareholders of the company in general meeting (s 312). However, this relates to the director's position as an officer of the company, and it

does not apply to money paid in settlement of contractual rights which a director may have by virtue of the termination of his service agreement.

- A director may not be given a service agreement for a term over five years, unless it is first approved by the shareholders of the company in general meeting. If approval is not obtained the term is unenforceable (s 319).

- A company is prohibited from entering into what are termed 'substantial property transactions' with its directors and persons connected with them, unless it obtains its shareholders' approval. A substantial property transaction is one involving property worth £100,000 or 10 per cent of the company's net asset value, whichever is the lower figure, subject to a minimum of £2000 (s 320).

- Section 330 contains a general restriction on loans to directors from the company. This section and those following it expand on this general prohibition (in the case of public companies and companies in the same group as a public company) to cover also 'quasi-loans', whereby financial arrangements are entered into with a third party which have the effect of indirectly providing credit facilities to the director, and credit transactions in which the company gives the director credit.

Are there any exceptions to the general restrictions on loans from the company?

Yes, there are some exceptions to permit:

- a loan to a director of a company (or its holding company) which does not exceed £5000;
- quasi-loans not exceeding £5000 which are to be repaid within two months;
- credit transactions not exceeding £10,000.
- loans to cover a director's expenses incurred in the course of his or her duties, not exceeding £20,000 in total, and subject to approval by the shareholders.
- certain transactions and housing loans entered into by a money-lending company in favour of its directors.

Must a director disclose his or her involvement in any such transaction?

Yes, because of various duties of disclosure:

- a director has a wide-ranging duty of disclosure to the company of involvement in any transaction to which the company may be a party.

This duty arises from statute by Section 317 of the Companies Act 1985, and almost invariably also from the Articles of the company.

- details of such transactions must be disclosed in the accounts.

Are there any sanctions for non-compliance with the restrictions on benefits?

Yes, all the directors must take care to see that these restrictions are not infringed. The sanctions are that:

- transactions in breach of the provisions may be liable to be set aside by the company;
- personal liability may attach to the directors who authorised such a transaction, as well as the director benefiting from it; and
- breach of some of the sections, most notably s 330, is a criminal offence, which may lead to imprisonment or a fine.

What is the basis of a director's authority?

A director's authority is derived from the company's constitution.

The articles will normally give the board of directors the power to manage the day-to-day business of the company, subject only to directions given by a resolution passed by the shareholders on a 75 per cent majority.

However, certain matters may be reserved to the discretion of the shareholders, eg where borrowings over a specified limit may not be undertaken by the directors without approval.

May the board delegate its powers?

Yes, if the articles so authorise, the board may delegate any of its powers to a committee of one or more directors, which then assumes that specific responsibility. In so delegating the board does not lose its general power to act in the particular matter.

Can a limited number of directors pass valid board resolutions?

Yes, provided due notice is given to all, but a number of directors (even a majority in number) cannot purport to pass valid board resolutions without giving notice of the meeting to the whole board. The directors must not exclude any of their number from meetings and a director always has a right to attend meetings. Business done at a meeting of which some directors had no notice or from which they were excluded is invalid.

What is the authority of the directors?

As with all agents, within the scope of the authority given to them by the board as a whole or by the articles, the directors may enter into contracts and other arrangements on behalf of the company, without taking any personal liability upon themselves.

What if a director acts outside his or her authority?

If a director acts outside his or her authority, outsiders reasonably relying upon his or her actions without knowing of the lack of authority will still be able to enforce their rights against the company, but the company may take legal action against the offending director for any losses suffered.

How are decisions of the board taken?

Major decisions must be made by a resolution of the board of directors, which may be passed at a meeting of the board or by the directors' signatures to a written resolution, but must in any event be passed in accordance with the procedural rules laid down by the company's articles. As the articles normally provide that a specified number of directors shall form a quorum, not all directors need usually attend board meetings. If a quorum is not prescribed by the articles, a majority of the board will be a quorum in the absence of some other established practice of the board. The articles may give a casting vote to the chairperson of the board in the case of a tied vote, or provide for the voting rights of certain directors to be given additional weight on particular matters.

How are the powers of a director restricted?

Many factors will affect the way in which a director exercises his or her powers. The main areas to be aware of are:

- shareholders' control or influence;
- common law duties; and
- statutory requirements.

How is control by the company's shareholders exercised?

Control by the company's shareholders is exercised through their ability to dismiss a director by resolution in a general meeting. Some articles impose a requirement for a proportion of the directors to retire at each annual general meeting and to stand for re-election if they wish to continue in office, but in practice (in particular in smaller companies) these provisions are frequently omitted.

Does reliance on shareholder control or influence cause difficulty?

Yes, problems can arise in small and large companies, although for different reasons. In small companies members of the board often hold large shareholdings and it may be impossible for a minority shareholder to compel the calling of an extraordinary general meeting. Even if such a general meeting is called, the minority shareholder may be overwhelmed by the voting rights, as shareholders, of the very directors whose conduct he or she is seeking to question.

In contrast, in large companies, particularly those quoted on the Stock Exchange, ownership may be spread very widely and there may consequently be little contact between the members. Accordingly, in the absence of substantial institutional shareholdings, it may be difficult to organise effective shareholder control of the directors.

What are the provisions relating to the duties of a director?

There are the general duties imposed on a director by common law which are:

- the duty of skill and care; and
- his or her fiduciary duties to the company.

These duties are complemented by statutory duties which impose separate responsibilities.

What is the duty of skill and care?

The duty of skill and care concerns the ability of the director as an officer of the company, and requires the director to do his or her job to the best of his or her ability. This duty is far from severe, and the degree of skill expected of a director is judged subjectively with regard, for example, to his or her qualifications. A director is not obliged as part of his or her duty of care to give continuous attention to the affairs of the company, although an executive director might well have this obligation imposed separately by his or her service agreement. It should be noted that the common law duty of skill and care is supplemented in particular by the Insolvency Act 1986, which imposes more rigorous standards on directors.

What are the fiduciary duties?

Fiduciary duties are those arising from the trust which is placed in a director by a company. The duties are owed by the director to the company only and not to the shareholders, either jointly or as individuals.

They include the following.

- A duty to act in good faith in the best interests of the company. This means directors must promote what they feel to be the commercial interests of the company to the best of their ability, and must try to balance both short-term and longer-term considerations.

- A duty to act for proper purposes. This means directors must not use their powers for purposes other than the pursuit of the company's objects. The issue of shares provides the most common example of 'improper purpose', ie where additional shares are issued by a board to adjust the voting position of the shareholders in general meeting and thereby to improve the position of the directors, rather than for the purpose of raising capital. This is *not* allowed, and a transaction contravening this principle may be ineffective.
- A duty to deal properly with the company's assets. The board has control of company assets and therefore is responsible for any dealing with the assets which is forbidden by the company's constitution, or is in conflict with the interests of the company.
- The director must avoid personal conflicts of interest. A director must avoid wherever possible taking part in any decision where his or her own personal interest or duty may conflict with the interests of the company. An extension of this principle is that the director should always notify the company of any interests in contracts which are being considered by the company.
- There is a duty not to make secret profits. Any profit acquired by reason of holding office as a director must be accounted for to the company, unless it has been disclosed to the company and the director has been authorised to keep it by the shareholders in general meeting.

What are the statutory provisions?
The director is subject to statutory requirements, including:

- under ss 311–344 of the Companies Act 1985 there are various restrictions and controls on benefits to directors (considered above), and on share dealings by directors, their families and associates;
- a general duty to have regard to the interests of the company's employees as well as its members (s 309 of the Companies Act 1985);
- the provisions of the Insolvency Act 1986 (considered below);
- under the companies legislation, directors are responsible for the maintenance of company records, and for the preparation and filing of the company accounts and annual returns, besides presentation of the annual accounts to the shareholders in general meeting. These records may be inspected by the members of the company, and some must be made public. Regulation of the provisions is by the Registrar of Companies who may impose sanctions on companies not complying.

Directors may, in some circumstances, incur personal liability for a company's non-compliance with the statutory requirements.

What about the additional obligations on directors of public companies?

The Companies Act 1985 imposes several additional obligations upon the directors of a public company. It is important to know that:

- a public company must have at least two directors, in contrast to a private company which need only have one;
- an expert's report is required where shares are to be issued for non-cash consideration;
- if a public company suffers a serious loss of capital, its directors must convene an extraordinary general meeting to report to the shareholders;
- in addition to the requirement that a company may only pay dividends out of profits available for the purpose, a public company may only do so where the payment does not reduce net assets to less than the aggregate of its called-up share capital, plus undistributable reserves;
- directors must retire at 70 years of age, unless the company chooses to exclude the requirement.

A director of a public company should also be aware of the rules on insider dealing, the provisions of the financial services legislation, the rules of the Stock Exchange and the City Code on Takeovers and Mergers.

What are the insider dealing rules?

The Companies Securities (Insider Dealing) Act 1985 makes it an offence for anyone who, by virtue of their position, holds 'unpublished price-sensitive information' in relation to any publicly traded shares (ie any financial information which is not known to the market as a whole and which would affect the value of the share being traded) from dealing in the company's securities or assisting others to do so. If dealing does take place then the person concerned will be liable to a fine or imprisonment under the Act.

What is the scope of the financial services legislation?

The Financial Services Act 1986 imposes detailed provisions for the protection of investors. Its principal purpose was the establishment of professional organisations to regulate different aspects of the financial services industry. Each of these organisations produces its own rules, which do not have the force of law, but breach of which can lead to disciplinary proceedings resulting in fines and the possible prevention of individuals and companies from conducting business.

However, the Act also contains a number of provisions which are particularly relevant to directors of companies whose shares are publicly traded, in particular concerning the advertising of investments and misleading statements regarding investments. These are often of concern in the context of takeover offers and public offerings of shares, where the Takeover Code and Stock Exchange Rules may also be relevant.

It is the Takeover Code and the Stock Exchange Rules, rather than the Companies Act and Financial Services Act, which govern the conduct of most takeovers and mergers in the UK. The Code, which comprises general principles and rules to be observed during the course of a takeover, does not carry the force of law, but there are strong incentives to comply with its requirements.

The Stock Exchange Rules lay down the procedure to be followed on the admission of a company to the official list of the Stock Exchange and set out the continuing obligations of listed companies, most importantly, rules relating to the disclosure of information which may have an impact on prices and/or trading in the listed companies. The rules also contain the Model Code relating to dealings by directors aimed at avoiding insider dealing and provisions governing acquisitions and takeovers.

Can a director be responsible for the acts of the company?
Yes, a director must be careful to ensure that both he or she and the company act lawfully. For example, recent developments concerning the responsibilities of companies for loss of life show that both the company itself and its directors can be charged with the offence of manslaughter.

Can a director delegate any of his or her responsibilities?
Yes, provided that the director has good grounds for believing the person to whom he or she delegates to be capable of fulfilling those responsibilities. If the director delegates properly then, unless he or she has reason to believe the delegate is not carrying out those responsibilities adequately, he or she will not be responsible for the negligence of the delegate.

What if some board members are lax about their responsibilities?
If an individual director feels that one or more of the directors may be in breach of any of the duties mentioned above, he or she should inform the board and request that professional advice be taken. If he or she is still concerned, for example if the other directors are unwilling to act, then the

director should him or herself seek professional advice to safeguard his or her own position.

What if a director is unsure about his or her own position?

Particularly where personal interest is concerned, a director should always make full disclosure to the board and consider seeking professional advice.

What are the potential consequences of a breach of duty by a main board director?

This depends on the duty breached, but liability at law can be either criminal or civil.

What about criminal liability?

Criminal liability is enforced by the authorities through the criminal justice procedure. Examples of the criminal offences particularly relevant to directors are those arising under the Companies Securities (Insider Dealing) Act 1985, fraud and the specific offences created by the Insolvency Act 1986.

How does civil liability arise?

Civil liability is the responsibility owed by one legal person to another where loss has been suffered. The chief concern for a director is his or her potential liability to the company. For example, if a director misapplies company assets, in breach of his or her fiduciary duties, the company has a right to recover the loss suffered from the director concerned.

Again, if a director enters into a contract outside his or her authority, it may have to be honoured by the company, unless the other party to the contract knew of the lack of authority and acted in bad faith, and the company may seek to recover any loss from the director.

If the directors carry on the company's affairs in a way which is unfairly prejudicial to some of its shareholders, then those shareholders may bring an action under s 459 of the Companies Act 1985 for an order to restore their position. In extreme circumstances, the court can order that the company be wound up.

Professional indemnity insurance for directors

Directors are entitled to look to the company in respect of all liabilities properly incurred by them in the management of the business of the company, but not in respect of wrongful acts committed by them.

However, actions against directors for failure to show the standard of care owed by them are becoming more common, and directors may now seek cover with insurers. The cover can be arranged in the name of the company with indemnities to the extent of such insurance being given to the named individuals.

Such insurance does not extend to fraud or dishonesty, criminal behaviour or similar, although the company can have separate fidelity insurance for its *own* risks in respect of the individuals it employs.

Can shareholders ratify the improper acts of directors?
The shareholders in general meeting have the power to ratify in the company's name some (but not all) acts done improperly or without authority.

What about the sanction of dismissal?
Yes, it must be remembered that directors are also employees of the company and their negligence or improper conduct may be a ground for termination of a lucrative service contract.

What are the consequences of a company insolvency for its directors?
A company is insolvent if it cannot pay its debts as they fall due, or if its total debts at any one time are greater than its total assets. Until the Insolvency Act 1986 and the Company Directors Disqualification Act 1986, the position of a company director who could not be proved to have been dishonest was relatively protected if his or her company became insolvent.

What is the effect on directors of the Insolvency Act 1986?
Section 214, which applies on the winding-up of an insolvent company, is of most relevance to directors. If it can be shown that at some time before the commencement of the winding-up a director (or a shadow director) knew or ought to have concluded that there was no reasonable prospect that the company would avoid going into insolvent liquidation, then the director may be liable to make whatever contribution the court orders to the assets of the company. The court will take into account the general knowledge and skill of the individual concerned and will look also to his or her areas of responsibility and particular qualifications.

Does this mean that a director's own position will be under threat if he or she feels that the company has passed the point of no return with regard to its debts but none the less allows it to carry on trading, causing loss to other parties?
Yes, if a director considers that insolvent liquidation is inevitable, he or she must inform the board and recommend immediate action, probably

involving the appointment of a professional insolvency practitioner to minimise loss. If the director is overruled by the board, he or she should take separate legal advice.

What is the aim of the Company Directors Disqualification Act (CDDA) 1986?

It was enacted to stop unsuitable persons from acting as company directors. Under the Act the court has the power to make disqualification orders for periods of up to 15 years.

What are the grounds for disqualification orders?

These are wide and include:

- the involvement of a director in wrongful trading under s 214 of the Insolvency Act 1986;
- persistent breaches of the companies legislation; and
- fraud in the conduct of a company's business or in winding-up proceedings.

What are the sanctions under the CDDA 1986?

- The prohibition itself, which is extremely wide. If an individual is subject to an order he or she is prevented from being a director, and also prohibited from being directly or indirectly concerned in the promotion or management of a company in any way.
- Personal liability without limit for all the company's debts if the prohibition is breached.
- And criminal penalties including two years' imprisonment and/or a large fine.

How does an individual cease to be a director other than through a court order?

Both as an officer of a company and as an employee, a director can:

- resign;
- retire; or
- be dismissed.

What if a director resigns?

A director may resign his or her office at any time, and he will cease to have any further duties and the necessary amendments must be made to the company's statutory records. Where an executive director is resigning he or she may, as an employee, have a period of notice to serve under the terms of his or her service agreement.

When does a director retire?
The articles may provide that a certain proportion of the directors must retire at each annual general meeting. If a director retires and does not stand for re-election, he or she automatically ceases to hold office. Retirement from employment, at or before retirement age, will lead to the mutual termination of any service agreement.

Is dismissal of a director difficult?
Yes, dismissal may be difficult. A director may be dismissed from his or her office by a resolution of a majority of the shareholders in general meeting. Special notice requirements apply to the meeting and the director has the right to speak in his or her defence, and circulate the shareholders in advance. In addition, the articles may sometimes provide that certain shares will have extra voting rights on a resolution for the dismissal of an officer of the company. Such a provision is usually included for the protection of directors owning a substantial minority holding.

What about dismissal of a director as an employee?
Dismissal as an employee may fall within the employment protection legislation. For example, the director may be dismissed by due notice being given, but may still be able to bring a claim for unfair dismissal or for redundancy under that legislation. If the employment is terminated early, a director may also be able to claim against the company for losses suffered due to breach of his or her service agreement, most obviously salary for the balance of the term of the agreement.

Are there any proposals for changes in the law which will affect directors?
There is currently under review an amended proposal for an EC fifth directive on the harmonisation of company law. This document includes measures which, if effected, would considerably change the structure and proceedings of public companies in the UK.

Although still under discussion it is worth summarising the main proposals of the directive. In particular the following is proposed:

- That all the directors of a company should bear joint and several liability for breaches of duty committed by one of their number, and a director should only be exonerated from this liability if he or she can prove that he or she was not at fault. This would reverse the current position in the UK where fault has to be proved against the individual to establish liability.

- That a 10 per cent minority of shareholders should have a right to issue proceedings in the company name in matters concerning directors' breach of duty. This proposal is likely to be adopted.
- That the board of directors should be obliged to meet at least once every three months.
- that the right of companies to create shares not carrying voting rights (except where the shares carry a special advantage such as a preference dividend) should be abolished. This would mean voting patterns would match the size of shareholdings.
- That abstentions by shareholders in general meeting should count as votes against the motion.
- Every public company would be obliged compulsorily to transfer 5 per cent of its profits into a statutory reserve until the reserve is equal to 10 per cent of its capital to provide a cushion against loss for creditors.

Are these proposals significant?

Yes. As the completion of the single European market results in more cross-border enterprises, while UK companies may not be forced to adopt the two-tier board system, they may well be required to fall progressively more in line with those in other member states, and directors may have to look to their liabilities in other member states. It should be stressed that the proposals are still under discussion.

What is the scope of product liability in the UK and who is responsible for it?

'Product liability' is a general term used to describe the responsibility of those involved in the manufacture or supply of goods for loss, damage or injury caused by their goods.

Until recently, a victim of defective goods often found it impracticable to establish fault without access to the manufacturer's or supplier's own records and materials. The EC addressed this problem by issuing the directive on product liability in July 1985 which imposed civil liability on producers in respect of defective products. This was based upon the principle of 'strict liability', ie the victim does not have to show fault on the part of the producer. If he or she can show that the injury, loss or damage was caused by a product, then the burden falls upon the producer to show a good reason why he or she should not be held responsible.

The EC directive was given effect within the UK by Part I of the

Consumer Protection Act 1987. Part II of the Act went on to consolidate and supplement existing provisions relating to consumer safety and to provide a new code of criminal liability. The civil rights granted under Part I of the Act are in addition to any right which may already exist under contract or negligence law. It should be noted, however, that the liability is imposed on the producer company rather than on the individual directors.

Primary liability under the Consumer Protection Act falls upon the producer of goods. However, there is also liability for persons putting their own name on products or using a trade mark and upon importers of goods into the EC. There is also liability for suppliers in limited circumstances.

Claims under the Act are limited to claims for death, personal injury, loss and damage to property (other than damage to the product itself). Economic loss only (such as loss of profits) cannot be recovered.

A number of defences are open to a person against whom a claim is made, including a defence to the effect that the state of scientific and technical knowledge at the relevant time did not enable the producer to discover the defect.

The time limit for bringing actions is somewhat tighter than under the Limitation Act 1980. The Act inserts into the Limitation Act 1980 a new section (s 11A) which provides for two alternative dates at which time begins to run, namely:

- three years from the date at which his action accrues, ie the date at which personal injury or significant property damage was first suffered by the plaintiff;
- three years from the date of the plaintiff's 'knowledge'. This is given different definitions under the Act depending on whether it relates to personal injury or property damage.

There is an ultimate long-stop clause provided for under the Act. The plaintiff's action is, irrespective of whether the time limits set out above have expired, extinguished ten years from the date at which the product was first put into circulation. This date will vary depending on whether the defendant is the producer, importer or supplier.

INDEX